WEASEL WORDS

Weasel Words

THE ART OF SAYING
WHAT YOU DON'T MEAN

by Mario Pei

HARPER & ROW, PUBLISHERS

NEW YORK, HAGERSTOWN,

SAN FRANCISCO,

LONDON

1817

Designed by Sidney Feinberg

Library of Congress Cataloging in Publication Data

Pei, Mario Andrew, 1901–1978
    Weasel words : the art of saying what you don't mean.
    Includes index.
    1. Vocabulary. 2. Semantics. 3. Mass media—United States. 4. Advertising—
United States. 5. English language—Vocabulary. I. Title.
P305.P4   422   76–5524
ISBN 0–06–013342–2

78 79 80 81 82 10 9 8 7 6 5 4 3 2

Contents

Weasel words. Words of convenient ambiguity, or a statement from which the original meaning has been sucked or retracted. Theodore Roosevelt popularized the term by using it in a speech in 1916 when criticizing President Wilson. A quotation from the speech provides a good example: "You can have universal training, or you can have voluntary training, but when you use the word *voluntary* to qualify the word *universal*, you are using a weasel word; it has sucked all the meaning out of *universal*. The two words flatly contradict one another."

Roosevelt was indebted to a story by Stewart Chaplin, "Stained-Glass Political Platform," which appeared in the *Century Magazine* in June 1900, and in which occurs the sentence: "Why, weasel words are words that suck the life out of the words next to them, just as a weasel sucks the egg and leaves the shell." In the U.S.A. a politician who sits on the fence is sometimes called a *weasler*.

*Brewer's Dictionary of Phrase and Fable
Centenary Edition*

WEASEL WORDS

1 The World of Weasel Words

A weasel word is defined in most of our comprehensive dictionaries as an equivocal word, one that is meant to deprive a statement of its force or evade direct commitment, one that retreats from taking a direct or forthright position.

The term, originating about 1900 and popularized by Theodore Roosevelt in 1916, was explained by him as follows: "When a weasel sucks an egg, the meat is sucked out of the egg; and if you use a weasel word after another, there is nothing left of the other."

This basic definition confers upon the weasel word an essentially negative or privative function. Words like "America," "democracy," "patriotism," "faith," "honesty," "integrity," through overuse and exaggeration, tend to lose some of their original value and semantic content, to the point where they are kicked around on all occasions, even when they have no connection with the topic under discussion.

In recent times, it has dawned upon our lexicographers that there is a creative, innovative variety of weasel word as well. The *Random House Dictionary,* for example, after going into the "evasive and ambiguous" definition, goes on to describe the weasel word as something that can be intentionally misleading; while *Webster's Third International* cites as one of its examples

Robert Littell, to the effect that the weasel word is "the adman's way of crossing his fingers behind his back when he makes a somewhat elastic statement."

Viewed in this light, the weasel word becomes part of the great historical process of language change, which is partly accidental, partly brought about by necessity, partly deliberate and purposeful. Ambiguity, the art of pulling punches, may remain foremost; but content is often added instead of being subtracted. Words are coined, constructions are created, meanings are added—as in the case of "gay," once an innocent word, more recently appropriated and flaunted by homosexuals, so that one is afraid to use it in its original meaning. (I suggested to the compiler of an English phrase book for Japanese tourists that it might be advisable to change "gay colors" to "brilliant colors".)

The weasel word is revealed in all its glory primarily in two fields of human activity, commercial advertising and politics. The latter is perhaps the one where the original definition of "emptied word" is most often seen, though advertising does not shrink from its use.

But these two primary fields have many important ramifications. Politics exists not only to push parties and candidates. It covers also the pushing of ideas and points of view, not necessarily connected with election campaigns. Commercial advertising is designed primarily to sell products. But it may also sell persons, by adding to their prestige and vogue (an ancient practice; Cicero, in a letter to a friend, says, *Valde te venditavi:* "I peddled you a lot"; in other words, "I gave you a big buildup," "I sold you to him").

For this reason, I feel justified in entering the first of the two most obvious fields (advertising and politics) along with others (such as sex, art and literature, science, education) that at first glance might seem to be only distantly related, but on closer inspection are found to have strongly publicitarian features of a weasely nature.

What should be our attitude and reaction with regard to weasel words? Are they to be viewed as a total loss to the language, a degenerative process that saps at the root of language and debases it? Are they an enhancement, an enrichment, to be viewed with favor? Should we consider them as an integral part of the vast, universal process of language change, which has been going on since the birth of language, and which we can do very little about?

Purists condemn weasel words, along with all change in what they choose to call the "standard language." Innovators and linguists of a liberal stripe view them with a measure of favor, as representing the linguistic reality of the moment. Both sides uphold their theses with an abundance of plausible arguments.

Practically speaking and in self-protection, we should at least be informed about weasel words, their implications, how they affect us. It is well to learn to recognize a weasel word when you see it, know who and what is behind it, and be in a position to protect yourself from the entrapments for which it was devised.

Many writers have called attention to words and uses of words that they consider evil. A few have pointed to the relativism of words; that is, the acquisition of semantic content according to the person or group that uses the identical word or expression. William F. Buckley, Jr., in his August 28, 1975, column, offers a perfect example: "Colossus of the North," an expression of fear and detestation used by some Mexicans when referring to the United States; but the same expression is used by Guatemalans in referring to *their* big and sometimes pushy northern neighbor—Mexico. Leonard Read, in his *Notes from FEE* of March 1975, presents other examples closer home: "laissez-faire," a term of abhorrence to followers of the Keynesian school, who read into it all the evils attributed to democratic capitalism, as against Read's own definition: "a fair field and no favor." "Capitalism" itself is to sincere Marxists a word redolent with dirt and crime; Washington and Wall Street would never agree. "Democracy," which was defined by Lincoln as "government of the people, by the people, for the people," is redefined by James Russell Lowell as "the bludgeoning of the people, by the people, for the people." (What, incidentally, is the opposite of "democracy"? "Aristocracy," "autocracy," "dictatorship," "people's republic"?) Raymond Williams in his *Keywords: a Vocabulary of Culture and Society,* points to "nationalism," a "good" word as applied to your own nation or group, a "bad" word if used by an annoying minority in your own national complex; in like manner, "national feeling" is "good," "nationalistic feeling" is "bad."

As against these words that depend for their meaning on the user, there are others that come close to having acquired a universally pejorative connotation ("bureaucracy," for example), and others that have fully achieved that unenviable status ("reactionary," "radical," "dirty tricks," "invisible government," "infiltration"). Closer to the old definition of a weasel word (one that obfuscates) are such commercial terms as "additive," "enriched," "huge," "jumbo," "the big quart"; political-economic terms like "inoperative," "defense program," "downward adjustment," "retrenchment"; educational terms like "underachiever," "to relate well with one's peer group"; sexual terms like "alternate life-style."

Nowhere in recent times has the weasel word been used to such good (or bad) advantage as in connection with our 1976 Bicentennial celebration. The commercial hoopla that attended it was approved, or at least tolerated, by the overwhelming majority; it was disapproved by a small but strident minority.

Interestingly, the latter group produced its own crop of weasel words. The alarm against the commercial aspects of the celebration was first sounded by a self-appointed People's Bicentennial Commission, backed by *The Nation* (January 10, 1976), which described the P.B.C. as something "to make

Americans aware of their critical heritage—and of the continued existence of the injustices that spawned the heritage." In the lengthy piece, readers were warned against "hucksters," their "over-priced, nonnutritious, red-white-and-blue cornflakes," "the sacred marriage of American democracy and American capitalism," something described as not yet in existence in 1776, historical indications to the contrary.

At the outset of the year, the Concord and Lexington ceremonies were disturbed by groups of noisy demonstrators with their signs of "BUY-centennial" and "PAY-triotism." The celebrations took this opposition in their stride, and long before July 4 it had subsided. The question is still open: "To what extent was it justified?" Was the Bicentennial really a BUY-centennial? (SELL-centennial might have been more appropriate.) To what extent is our American society based on the deliberate use of words to mislead hearer or reader, whether for commercial, political, or prestige purposes?

Historically, as far back as records can take us, festivals have been the occasion for the buying, selling, and exchange of products. National and religious holidays, country fairs, world fairs, expositions have invariably been used for commercial purposes. Princes, kings, popes, leaders of all types and descriptions have regularly lent their presence and efforts to the commercial success of such celebrations. It was President William Howard Taft who said, "I have come to the conclusion that the major part of the work of a President is to increase the gate receipts of expositions and fairs and bring tourists into the town." Frances Trollope, in 1832, said, "Nothing can exceed their [Americans'] activity and perseverance in all kinds of speculation, handicraft and enterprise, which promises a profitable pecuniary result." This leads one commentator to remark, "After all, it's the American way," and another to say, "The Bicentennial is criticized for being commercial. But if it weren't, wouldn't it be a bit un-American?" A humorist adds, "Some want the Bicentennial to be meaningful, others want it to be fun, and still others want to make a buck. Well, at least they're all good American objectives." But Horace Sutton deplores overstress on what he calls the "Bicenetcetera," and further reminds us that Costa Carras, of the new breed of Greek shipowners, though he speaks cultivated Oxonian English, insists on pronouncing "Byzantine" as "BUY-zantyne."

Yet there is such a thing as measure and good taste. Fire hydrants painted with the national colors are not in good taste, when one considers the double function of such hydrants. The amount of trinkets, souvenir buttons, medals, coins, useless mementos of all kinds, sold through an appeal to the spirit of patriotism, was beyond all reasonable bounds.

The commercial usage that most distressed me in the course of the year was the constant radio-TV appeal to "America" in connection with commercial offerings. ("America! See what we got!"; "We're the third largest coffee in America!"; etc., ad nauseam.) Perhaps I am oversensitive, but to me it seemed like a desecration of a once hallowed name.

2 Weasel Word Transmission Channels

How are weasel words propagated and popularized so that they can enter and affect the language? Word-of-mouth is the most ancient and traditional transmission channel. The word is coined or semantically modified by someone who has prestige or status in the community. It is picked up by his admiring followers, used by them, and sometimes quickly becomes part of the common language. Many of the proverbs and sayings that have come down to us from the days of the Hebrews, Greeks, and Romans contain weasely features that have been perpetuated, even if their nature is no longer recognized. The oral form of transmission is still in use today among groups that have not yet escaped the bonds of illiteracy.

The invention of writing gave language, and its burden of weasel words, a permanency that has become accepted and time-honored. But even the greatest of the ancient and medieval civilizations could boast, at the most, of a bare 20 percent literacy. It was Gutenberg's invention of the printing press, coupled with the extension of education to the formerly illiterate, that made the written language the biggest and best conveyor of language innovations, both good and bad.

It remained for the twentieth century to devise substitutes for the written language, which in the view of some may eventually lead to the obliteration of reading and writing. Many educators, startled by the degeneration of our schools, express the fear that this process may already be in motion. The great modern substitutes for language in written or printed form are the visual and auditory media, radio and television, which tend to usurp the function of books, magazines, and newspapers.

People of my generation well remember the days, down to the end of World War I, when if you wanted the latest news you had to buy an extra edition of a newspaper. If you wanted information of a more permanent kind, you had to get it out of books. If you wanted entertainment, you had your choice of theaters, vaudeville shows, silent movies, books, and magazines, even of the dime variety.

Today, things are vastly different. News, information, entertainment can bypass the written language and reach you through the ear, courtesy of radio, or through a combination of ear and eye, by means of television. There is one essential difference: reading, even of trash, calls for some participation of the conscious brain and for certain processes that may be styled intellectual. The printed page, which is a symbol of spoken language, has to be conveyed through the eyes to the brain centers, where the linguistic symbolism is transformed into the appropriate imagery that reflects the ultimate reality, true or fictional, that the writer is trying to convey to his reader. But radio can be absorbed through the ear with only one transformation, from spoken language to mental image; while the TV viewer can refrain from exercising his brain, and absorb, through ear and eye, the complete image that is meant for him. This means that the new media are ideal for propaganda, whether commercial or political. They can not only spread weasel words and expressions already in circulation; they can create them outright, which is precisely what they do. They are weasel word carriers and incubators par excellence. The passivity of the radio listener and TV viewer is highly favorable to the weasel word. The critical, discriminating function of the conscious brain, which is stimulated by the reading process, is lulled to sleep by radio listening and TV viewing. Commercial advertisers and politicians are well aware of this feature, and use it to the full and to their own advantage.

Is all this going to affect the coming generations? Here is the prophecy of one of the foremost practitioners of TV art, Paddy Chayevsky: "Of course it affects the kids. TV will bring about genetic changes. Our eyes will become bigger. In two thousand years we'll lose our legs, having no further use for them. And we'll have very big ears." And he adds, "TV is democracy at its ugliest. Give the people what they want!"

But the written language, despite the lugubrious predictions of Marshall McLuhan and his cohorts, shows no signs of an early demise. Despite the rivalry of the new media, perhaps even because of it, there is a proliferation of written material of all descriptions. The book industry flourishes, both in hardcover and in paperback, far more than in the past. Newspapers, though to a lesser degree than earlier in the century, are still in abundant circulation. The same is true of magazines, despite deterioration of quality. In railroad, bus, and airline terminals, in public places of all kinds, written signs, often in more than one language, flank the voice of the loudspeaker. Above all, there are the endless reams of written material issued by and for the all-pervasive bureaucracy of the modern state, as well as to satisfy the requirements of big industry and big business. The written media are all there, continuing and expanding their functions of earlier centuries, and these include the recording and spreading of language innovations, good and bad; particularly of weasel words and expressions. Of this, commercial and political interests with axes to grind are fully conscious. Accordingly, they make abundant use of the written media. The advertising matter and political messages that come to us through the written language are worthy rivals of those carried by the new media. Such at least is the state of affairs in countries that have achieved a high degree of modern mechanical civilization.

Of course, there is plenty of overlapping between the older press media and the newer radio-TV. Commercially, printed ads in the first often duplicate spoken and visual advertising in the second. Politically, candidates' speeches are first carried on radio-TV, then reproduced, often without condensation, in newspapers and magazines. Occasionally the process is reversed. The content or message is what counts. The weasely aspects, where they appear, seldom vary from one medium to the other.

But there are also significant differences in the way one medium lends itself to weaselism better than another. "BUY-" and "PAY-centennial" work out well on TV, where a picket sign is flashed on the screen, and in the press, where they are spelled out; not so well on radio, where they have to be described and explained. A smirk, a gesture, a facial expression of astonishment, wonder, admiration, disgust are ideal for TV; difficult, not to say impossible, for the press (unless accompanied by a lucky photo) or for radio. A message that involves figures and statistics, save on the simplest plane, is best reserved for the press. But all this is well known to both advertising agencies and political committees. Weasel words, expressions, complete messages are distributed accordingly.

There is also coincidence and confusion of old and new media in the spreading of vogue words that may not themselves be weasely, but lend themselves to weasely use. Consider, for example, "charisma," applied to the field of politics (who would have dreamed of applying it to a candidate for office before the time of John F. Kennedy?). Or "clout," originally a heavy blow, even in the earlier slangy sense of "pull"? "Escalate" was given vogue by the Vietnam War, though it existed in a different sense long before it. "Communicate" is an old word; in the sense in which it is used in educational circles, along with the ineffable "learning in depth," it is recent. "Guesstimate," or "educated guess," "feedback," "input," "specificity" are creations of various fields of science, extended beyond their original borders.

One feature of all advertising, commercial and political, of which the general public is acutely unaware is that its cost is borne not by the advertisers but by the consuming public itself. In commercial advertising the cost is simply added to the ultimate price paid by the consumer, either on the price tag of the product or (with a political link) by the full deductibility of advertising costs on corporation returns, which has to be made up for either by additional taxation on individual returns or, invisibly but no less painfully, by currency inflation, which is reflected in the cost of living of every man, woman, and child.

In the political field, the cost of advertising is ultimately borne by the voter-consumer. In the bad old days before Watergate, large contributors to political campaigns (and this includes both big corporations and big labor unions) bore the ostensible cost. The corporations reimbursed themselves by seeking and obtaining legislation favorable to their corporate interests, such as government contracts, high tariffs, price supports, export bounties, which went to raise prices to the consumer. The labor unions sought and found their reward in labor legislation designed to increase the perquisites of union members and their leaders, and boost prices to the consumer.

Today, big political contributions, in the tens and hundreds of thousands of dollars, are outlawed. But individual contributions in smaller amounts are still permissible. It is simply a matter of making it plain to corporation employees and union members that they should make, in their own interest, such individual contributions, which the government matches, dollar for dollar, out of the one dollar set aside in your tax return for the purpose of nonpartisan financing of political campaigns. How many taxpayers who check the box permitting one dollar of their tax to go for that purpose realize that that dollar is subtracted from what is available for other government activities, and has to be made up for, as usual, either by additional taxation or by currency inflation, both of which are harmful to him or her as an individual and as a consumer?

But all this is a mere introduction. Our main and immediate concern is with the way in which advertising and publicity, with all their branches and appendages, pollute the language in trying to achieve their ends.

3 Radio and TV—Merits

It is only fair that first honors should go to the most modern, most scientifically constructed of our weasel-word vehicles—what someone has styled "the electronic press."

The wide application of radio as a public conveyor of information, entertainment, and commercial publicity goes back to the 1920s. Acting as an agent for a new weekly, I was among the first to prepare commercial scripts for New York's early WJZ and WEAF. Radio, in part—but only in part—displaced an earlier invention, the phonograph. Today, disc jockeys have brought about a happy marriage of the two.

Television came in later, as a home substitute for the earlier movies, which, like the phonograph, were only partly displaced. Of all the media, TV is probably the most pervasive. It has insinuated itself into practically every American home. There are more TV sets than bathtubs in existence. TV antennae can be seen rising from hovels that lack running water. Where power lines are nonexistent, portable batteries supply the juice for the TV set. More homes boast of two or more TV sets than of two or more cars.

In its own way, TV is also the most insidious of all the spreaders of entertainment, information (misinformation, if you prefer), and propaganda, both commercial and political. It requires little or no use of the conscious mind, only receptive eyes and ears. It calls for practically no physical exertion. You don't have to walk or drive or be driven, as is the case with the movies; just turn a switch, often portable and held in your hand, sink into your favorite armchair, open your eyes and ears, and shut off your brain (the last, however, is optional; you may keep it turned on if you want to exercise it critically). It is no wonder that such unflattering expressions as "boob tube" have been coined for it. It is no wonder that the only thing that has saved conventional movies from extinction is the fact that there is normally a considerable time lag between the first appearance of a new movie in theaters where you pay admission and its release for TV use, where the cost to the viewer in terms of electric power, purchase price of a set, and repair costs, along with higher prices for the products advertised, are disguised or deferred.

Parents, educators, and writers are distressed over the fact that children spend long hours viewing TV instead of reading or learning how to read. But the same parents who deplore what their children do are most often guilty of the same practices. The situation is nationwide and, as living standards improve in many nations, tends to become worldwide.

Before examining TV as a conveyor of commercial and political propaganda and weasel words, it may be useful to dissect its general characteristics, both good and bad.

Outside of commercials, TV's output, like Caesar's Gaul, may be divided into three parts: First, newscasts and documentaries, which continue the newsreel and occasional travelogue of pre-TV movies; but with the added good feature of immediacy, for the newscast often picks up the news item on the spot, as it happens, and, through ultramodern Telstar and space satellites, from all over the world. Second, cultural programs, such as plays, operas, concerts, ballet, etc. These were only occasionally presented in pre-TV movies, though they were always available through the simple expedient of walking or driving to the theater or concert hall and paying admission. People incapacitated by reason of age, health, location and mobility, or financial status are now in a position to enjoy these offerings without moving from their homes or hospital beds. Third, fictional offerings, ranging all the way from soap operas and situation comedies to Westerns, police stories, war episodes, criminal activities, with their frequent attendant display of violence, and ultra-risqué pictures verging on the pornographic (the most porno of the last-named have not yet made it to the TV screen, but they are getting there fast—witness the storm of protests over the situation comedy "Soap"). These fictional offerings were, and still are, the backbone of the old motion pictures; they, too, are available to shut-ins and children. In connection with the latter, it is easier to exclude a child viewer from a certain type of picture in a theater than it is to cut him or her off from the same picture on TV without careful and constant parental supervision, "family hours" notwithstanding. Correspondingly, TV viewing is blamed, rightly or wrongly, for tendencies to violence and sexual promiscuity that are rampant in today's younger generations ("rightly or wrongly" calls for a fuller explanation that will be forthcoming in the next chapter). Also, on the plus side, it must be admitted that a great many TV programs, whether or not child-slanted, supply the young with valuable information of all kinds, and, if proper selectivity is exercised, even with highly cultural material.

TV brings to its newscast viewers what is actually going on, as it happens. If there are "obstreperous, objectionable" demonstrations by "misguided" groups, you see them, and judge their merits accordingly. If there is "police brutality," you witness it in action. You hear spokesmen for both sides of highly controversial issues. You are able to make up your own mind as an eyewitness concerning the merits of the issue and the way it is handled. This is much better than reading about it in the paper and getting the sometimes biased, sometimes accidentally distorted views of a press reporter.

TV alone is able to show you, on the screen, certain situations that involve minorities and racial groups both as they exist and as they ought to exist. On TV today there are almost as many women newscasters and commentators, at least on local stations, as there are men. These women are thoroughly professional and effective. What man in his right mind would object to them? The news staffs include plenty of blacks, Hispanics, and other minorities, roughly in proportion to the numbers of these groups in the general population. They are, without exception, alert, efficient, pleasant, well-spoken. One would have to be a dyed-in-the-wool racist not to like them. Does this not constitute a highly valuable contribution to our avowed national policy of equality and integration?

The fictional programs are occasionally criticized on the ground that they present certain ethnic groups in an unfavorable light. This has been in part corrected. On the other hand, consider the large number of blacks, Orientals, American Indians, Italians, Slavs who are cast in a highly favorable light in fictional offerings of the type of "Ironside," "The Rookies," "Mod Squad," "Police Story," "Baretta," "Hawaii Five-O." Too fictional? The records of our police departments indicate that this type of fiction is paralleled in real life.

Radio, with its simple auditory message, is an even greater equalizer than TV. Leontyne Price as Leonora in *Forza del Destino* might strike some TV viewers as strange, as might also in the same opera Calatrava's objection to Alvaro as being of mixed white and Indian blood. But on radio there is no color line, only vocal excellence.

On the purely cultural side, the potentialities of radio and TV are tremendous. Unfortunately, they are exploited only in part. But even so, when one thinks of the ease with which a concert, a ballet, a good play can be reached on either medium, one must bless the new media. AM-FM radio programs of a cultural, truly adult variety are both plentiful and frequent. TV educational channels are available in many localities, and are often utilized by schools and colleges. New Jersey Public Television often puts on a "TV for Learning" week, which is offered in the classrooms, with mathematics, physics, social sciences, English, foreign languages, history, civics presented directly to the schoolchildren through the medium they have learned to love best. When I was visiting professor at the University of Pittsburgh, in 1962–1963, the local educational channel enlisted my cooperation for an elaborate series of programs in which we presented, both for the colleges and high schools and for direct area home consumption, "The Languages of the World," complete with lectures, music and songs, and native speakers. The tongues ranged not only over Western and Eastern Europe, including the Soviet Union, but as far away as the Arab countries, Israel, Turkey, Iran, India, China, Japan, Korea, and Vietnam. Also included were Black Africa (Swahili and Hausa), some native tongues of South America (Quechua, Tupi-Guaraní), the Pacific island world of Indonesia and the Philippines (Malay-Indonesian and Tagalog), Hawaii, Samoa, New Zealand (Maori). The program was so successful that the tapes were requested by the State Department for presentation abroad. Unfortunately, they had already been erased for reuse by the time the request came.

TV documentaries have sometimes been described as a "dying" format (the Nielsen ratings, you know; a program describing our armed forces and national guard running second to "Holmes and Yo-Yo"; Luigi Barzini's documentary on present-day Italy behind "What's Happening"). We are also reminded of two splendid documentaries, one on ancient Rome, the other on the conquest of Mexico, produced by John Secondari for ABC-TV and never repeated. But to every rule there is an exception. CBS's "Sixty Minutes" and "Who's Who," NBC's "Weekend," ABC's "Special Edition," skillfully conducted by Barbara Feldon, are there to show that documentaries can hold their own even against fictional offerings if they are pushed hard enough. In the words of Bill Granger, "The documentary is dead. Long live it!"

Lastly, there are the good causes that are so often sponsored on radio-TV, both in newscasts and elsewhere—a disadvantaged family in dire need, a little boy from India who needs an expensive operation to restore his health. The situation is visually portrayed on the screen, the need is described by the newscaster, and the money to take care of the situation pours in from thousands of charitable viewers.

There are pictures that teach viewers, both young and old, to love and care for our mistreated environment (series like "Sierra" and Jacques Cousteau come to mind); others that teach their viewers to love and care for animals instead of seeing them with destructive eyes ("Animal World," the Patsy Awards). Many of these good features are duplicated in the press. But the power of the visual medium, the eyewitness feature, is largely specific to TV.

4 Radio and TV—Demerits, Real and Fancied

Outside of the quality and distribution of the ubiquitous commercials, which we will discuss in Chapter 7, what's wrong with TV?

The mildest among the criticisms has to do with the arrangement and placing of programs. One viewer bemoans the fact that the programs he likes are bunched up on two or three nights a week, when they are in direct conflict with one another, while there is a wasteland of at least three nights a week, "so that even a lousy show will get top ratings by default." This is partly a matter of individual tastes (some of the programs he describes as "super" cut no ice with me). But he seems to have his finger on the pulse when he alludes to the ratings war that goes on ceaselessly among the channels. (One instance that struck me was the night when two channels put on three-hour documentaries that interested me, one on "The Rise and Fall of the Third Reich," the other on "The Great Energy Problem," anchored by Walter Cronkite. They coincided for two and a half hours; I was kept shifting channels for the duration.) To the extent that the comparative ratings are designed to attract the advertisers, this partly moves the problem into the commercials field, and out of the area of intrinsic quality. It would be in the viewer's interest if the channels were to enter into some sort of collusion designed to keep significant programs of the same general nature out of conflict, regardless of the ratings. But I know this is too much to ask for.

The war for top ratings among the three leading TV networks leads columnist John Camper to accuse them of chicanery in trying to hook viewers onto their programs and keep them from switching and "channel swimming." Under the heading of "stunting," he offers three common practices: "cross-pollination" (putting the star of one series on an early episode of another series); "front-loading" (making the initial episode of a series particularly exciting, thus arousing expectations that fall short of achievement in later, cheaper, more humdrum episodes; this is often accompanied by "doubling" the length of the first episode, thus keeping you away from other networks for an extra thirty or sixty minutes); "cliff-hanging" (splitting a show into two parts, building the first part up to a climax, and leaving you hanging, *Perils of Pauline* style). He goes on to describe a change of title, such as "The Million Dollar Rip-off " in the place of "The Great Chicago Rip-off," as designed to keep viewers from thinking it's a documentary.

Time was when the great Sunday interview programs (CBS's "Face the Nation," NBC's "Meet the Press," ABC's "Issues and Answers") were properly spaced at eleven-thirty, noon, and twelve-thirty, respectively. More recently, they have often been placed, deliberately or accidentally, in direct confrontation in the same time slot. More "channel swimming" for interested viewers.

Columnist Marvin Kitman deplores laugh shows where there is nothing to laugh at, but plenty of laughing noises from the studio audience, on cue, "sometimes even before." He, too, has his individual tastes. He didn't laugh at "When Things Were Rotten," which I found highly entertaining. Also, he might have gone on to speak of the laugh track and its braying noises when there is no studio audience.

Sandor Vanocur presents a general indictment of humor on TV, which he thinks is planned mostly for teenagers. He concludes, somewhat callously: "Certainly there's a place for teenagers on TV. Also, there's a place for them elsewhere. Only the restraints imposed on writing for a family newspaper prohibit one from suggesting where that elsewhere might be."

More serious are complaints about endless violence and bloodshed on TV, which the American Medical Association's board of trustees has called "an environmental hazard" and "a risk factor which threatens the health and welfare of young Americans."

Dr. M. A. Rothenberg, a child psychologist, claims that the average American youngster will have seen eighteen thousand murders by the time he graduates from high school, and links the steady diet of violence on TV to widespread juvenile crime. In a somewhat lighter vein, columnist John Camper, having listed all the cop shows ("McCloud," "Columbo," "Forrester," "Baretta," "Kojak," et al.), and added to them private investigators ("Switch," "Cannon," "Harry O," etc.), comes up with a sum total of over seventeen hours a week of televised crime, including an average of forty killings, thirty beatings, and innumerable violations of civil rights. "It does get a bit monotonous, but apparently that is what a certain type of audience wants," he somewhat hopelessly concludes.

The California Medical Association accuses TV of being harmful to children in three ways: First, they learn and remember—and many copy—aggressive behavior. Second, it is easier for them to be violent, and they are less anxious about it. Third, it heightens, rather than "drains off," their aggressiveness.

The late actor Peter Finch, commenting on Chayevsky's film *Network*, claimed that it had a definite message about the potential evils of TV, which "caters to the lowest common denominator and trains us not to think"; his fourteen-year-old son, he went on, knows more about Angie Dickinson than about

George Washington; "TV has given him a packaged brain." The Reverend Jesse Jackson, one of the nation's most respected black leaders, remarks that twenty years ago life revolved around three centers—home, church, and school. The first gave discipline; the second, moral values; the third, information. Now TV and radio are the primary conveyors of both information and ethos; but they have the power without the responsibility. It's up to the parents, he concludes, to see that radio and TV, as well as the phone, are off every night from seven to nine, which should be homework time.

There is a reaction of sorts to the flood of TV-radio violence. A study conducted by the J. Walter Thompson Advertising Agency indicates that excessive TV violence may be detrimental to the advertiser. Ten percent of the people polled decided to boycott the products advertised on "violent" programs. But the study went farther, and produced a documentary film entitled *The Desensitization of America,* which considers the escalation of both sex and violence not only on TV but also in movies, pop music, and magazines, and reminds us that our young people were brought up in the violence-sex tradition, which may to some extent be traced back to a period of wars and assassinations that give fictional violence a highly realistic model.

It might be further remarked that all through the period ranging from the outset of World War II to the end of the Vietnam War, violence, both of a military nature and in connection with espionage activities, was presented in a highly favorable light, since it was in a "good" cause. Killing people in a commando raid, murdering secret operatives of a hostile power, bomb-throwing and kidnapping were not merely justified but glorified—on stage, screen, radio, TV, and in the press. It is to be wondered that once the "Good Cause" faded or failed, the practice lived on and was rationalized in weak minds that considered their own personal causes, fraught with hatred or acquisitiveness, to be just and legitimate?

Also, not everybody agrees with the thesis that radio-TV have the destructive influence described above. One Ann Landers correspondent writes: "Is it better to have your husband home watching TV than to wonder if he is out with another woman, down at the bar getting drunk, or at a gambling place losing his badly needed paycheck? Is it better to have your son at home in front of the boob tube than to wonder if he is out smoking dope, drunk behind the wheel of a car, committing vandalism, or maybe even mugging and raping? Your daughter can't get into too much trouble at home, glued to the idiot box." She goes on to add: "Two thousand years ago, a woman cut off John the Baptist's head and put it on a platter. Herod had a sword run through all male children under two years of age. An angry mob put a crown of thorns on Jesus' head and nailed him to a cross. None of them got the idea from watching TV." (Ann's comment: "The networks will love you!")

From another angle, columnist David Broder disputes the contention that the many hours spent before the TV set have to be stolen from something, specifically the development of intellectual skills. He holds that youngsters have an infinite capacity for wasting time, with or without the magic screen, and cites as a horrible example his eldest son, six years old before the family could afford a set, who nevertheless frittered away as much time as any of his younger, TV-nurtured brothers, and emerged as academically indolent as those who had had Howdy Doody from babyhood.

Nevertheless, such organized parent-teacher groups as the New Jersey Coalition for Better TV Viewing are coming into being to protect children both from too much TV violence and too much time spent on TV viewing.

On the terminological side, Marvin Kitman uses two new terms in connection with the frequent violent wrecking of automobiles on TV. One is "carology," the science of handling and wrecking cars on TV; the other is "to total," to make a total wreck out of a car. It seems that some people get a vicarious thrill from watching a car and its supposed occupants hurtle down a cliff and catch fire, when these same viewers would be horrified at the thought of getting a scratch, let alone a dent, on their own cars. In like manner, some people rush to the scene of an accident or fire, often obstructing attempts at rescue. They love to watch the blood darkening the waters in *Jaws,* though they would carefully refrain from wetting their feet in shark-infested waters. They love to watch someone contemplating suicide by jumping from a window ledge, and even urge him to jump. Attention is called to a new game in some theater lobbies, called "Death Race," where you insert a quarter, then run down all the "pedestrians" you can hit with your "car." Each time you zap another one, there's a simulated shriek, and a gravemarker appears on the screen. The National Safety Council calls this game "insidious, morbid," and "sick, sick, sick." But it's a top moneymaker. All the people described above are thrill-seekers, but, interestingly, always vicariously. It shouldn't happen to them to be on the receiving end.

If it is any consolation to critics of modern ways, such people have always existed. In ancient Rome, they loved to see the gladiators fighting each other to death, and Christians being thrown to the lions, but from the safety of their sheltered bleachers. In the Middle Ages, they thronged to the town square to witness a hanging, or a drawing and quartering. There is even today a popular Italian joking reply when someone remarks that it's a lovely day: "Yes, indeed! Too bad no one is being hanged!" In the French Revolution, the *tricoteuses* knitted as heads rolled under the guillotine. Today, the same sort of people love to watch bullfights, cockfights, prizefights, hockey fistfights. Is there any cure for them? Luckily, their number seems to be slowly dwindling, as we grow more humanitarian.

One disturbing question, however, remains to plague us. Is TV violence merely a reflection of what goes on in real life, as some claim? Or does life tend to draw inspiration from violence on TV? Or do the two merely reinforce each other in a sort of vicious circle? To this triple alternative, there seems to be, as yet, no definitive answer.

A third major criticism, of a more political nature, links TV directly with the older media. "Freedom of the press" is invoked every time a newspaper is accused of speaking out of turn, or of slanting the news to suit its editorial policy. The same privilege is claimed by TV reporters and newscasters, as indicated in the case of Daniel Schorr and his leak of restricted information to a press organ that gave it full publicity.

Still another criticism hinges on the mode of delivery and the political outlook of TV newscasters and commentators. Some, like CBS's Walter Cronkite, appear in both functions, with what might be described as a change of personality from the one to the other. In his late afternoon daily commentary on CBS-radio, Cronkite strikes many listeners as pompous, pretentious, and puffed up. He has even been nicknamed "The Oracle." In his evening TV newscast, on the other hand, he projects a gracious, grandfatherly image, highly attractive to the majority of his viewers. The oracular function was turned over to Eric Severeid, before his retirement, who, without sounding pompous, nevertheless managed to assume enough of the Voice of Authority to have earned the nickname of "Eric Sayitright."

It is admittedly difficult for the true political commentator, as distinguished from the newscaster, to keep his own (or his station's) views out of his commentary. Special time slots are allotted to so-called editorials, with an invitation to viewing dissenters to request time for their dissenting views, something which is regularly done. On the surface, we have all the trappings of democracy. In reality, there is little question that the opinions expressed by the official commentator or editorialist carry more weight with the average viewer or listener. When Nixon resigned under fire, it was the almost unanimous opinion of the commentators that losing the Presidency was punishment enough, and that no further action should be taken against him. When Ford issued his pardon, there was a sudden reversal. It is difficult to avoid the conclusion that this change in attitude was politically motivated. The change in attitude apparently spread to the general public, and was reflected in the 1974 congressional elections. To what extent we owe our top-heavy Democratic Congress to our commentators is a matter of conjecture.

Nevertheless, a study of the influence of TV on political campaigns and the voters' awareness of issues (*The Unseeing Eye,* by T. E. Patterson and R. D. McClure of Syracuse University) comes to the conclusion that people learn more about political issues from the press than from TV. The reason, according to the authors, is that while the press concentrates on issues and qualifications, TV favors hoopla (rallies, motorcades, polls, strategies). Support for this view came from the televised debates between Carter and Ford before the 1976 election. While the League of Women Voters, which sponsored the debate, insisted that the spotlight be kept exclusively on the debaters and the panel of questioners, the networks wanted freedom to shift to the studio audiences in order to televise their reactions. This was not in accord with the precedent set in the Kennedy-Nixon debates of 1960, and lent itself to the possibility of a biased audience that would, by its attitude, influence the millions of home viewers.

5 Additional Demerits

There is a wide assortment of additional criticisms of TV-radio. Eliot Wild, in the *Newark Star-Ledger,* accuses the networks of distorting their newscasts on behalf not of quality news but of higher ratings. Picturesquely, he describes the average two-hour newscast as a "two-hour newsburger with 45 minutes of news wrapped in a soggy bun of 'human interest,' 'lifestyle,' and 'people' features," and as "three per cent depth buried in prime-time schedules of pure marshmallow." When a TV executive calls for a "brighter, fresher package" in his station's newscasts, this is a notorious euphemism for "higher ratings." Another euphemism is "light, bright stories." My own observations coincide to some extent with Wild's, but I wonder whether this may not be a matter of taste. Commercial TV tries to appeal to all viewers, across broad cultural and educational bands. Yet, by and large, it does not seem to neglect news items of true significance. If more of these are desired, one can always turn to the local educational channel.

Another criticism, of a more mechanical nature, deals with movies, Hollywood-made and televised or specifically produced for TV use, where the background noises and/or music drown out the conversation. Also, there are unintelligible whispers and gasps, particularly in deathbed scenes, all in the name of realism.

While this item is discussed in greater detail in Chapter 10, there is a related criticism voiced by such columnists as Sandor Vanocur about the nonstop prattling of TV commentators in the course of televising such spectacles as President and Mrs. Carter's walk down Pennsylvania Avenue after the 1977 inauguration, and, even more strongly, the excessive verbiage of sports commentators like Howard Cosell when describing sports events. These commentators, says Vanocur, receive generous compensation for exhibiting their excitement when confronted with the obvious, and simply offend the viewers.

In this connection, I have a little gripe of my own in which I am sure the majority of viewers will not concur. When a foreign personality like Brezhnev or Giseard D'Estaing is speaking in his own language, why must everything but his first two or three words be completely smothered by the English translation? I'd like to hear what he has to say exactly as he says it, with all the semantic nuances. But I am fully aware that in this matter I am *vox clamantis in deserto.*

The predominance of color TV is said to be responsible for such titles as "The Girl in the Green Dress," "The Man in the Brown Suit." But this is rather a statement than a criticism.

Ernest Cuneo protests against the coverup that networks conduct of their own scandals, of the nature of which Chayevsky has given us some idea in *Network,* even while fully reporting, often with gusto, everyone else's scandals. He adds: "The government and people are powerless to censor the news. However, the networks censor the news practically every hour on the hour, by simply throwing into the waste-basket items they prefer that the American people doesn't hear." This, of course, is also a favorite practice of the press, which often relegates to page 34 a news item just as important as the ones featured on page 1, or omits it altogether, as has been frequently demonstrated by *Accuracy in Media.* This time, however, we have a political motivation rather than the economic one deplored by Eliot Wild.

Yet the importance of unbiased news, if at all achievable, is strongly advocated by Stanley Milgram of the City University of New York in *Antioch Review,* reprinted in *The New York Times* under the title "Confessions of a News Addict." Since our civilization is commercially oriented, he says, in substance, we purchase and ingest the products of the news industry with the same insatiable appetite that inspires us to buy consumer products. But the news, printed or televised, is becoming more and more a form of entertainment rather than a source of information. We demand that it be thrilling and exciting, at the same time that we feel obligated to know what is going on. The media know this, and respond accordingly. "If the news went away," Milgrim wonders, "would the world be any worse for it?"

Lastly, New York's Public Broadcasting System station, Channel 13, under the title "You Should See What You're Missing," presented in the closing days of 1976 a symposium of ten network professionals (producers, writers, researchers), who were asked what was wrong with TV. Interestingly, executives from the major networks, to a man, refused to appear on the program. Here are some of the charges, in condensed form: "Selling time is paramount. To this end, make a star glamorous at all costs." "Picayune censorship of scripts." (Obviously from a writer.) "Try to please everybody, avoid all controversy, even at the cost of producing pap." "Too much gratuitous violence for the purpose of catching attention." "A preference for popularity at the expense of quality." (From a researcher.) "There are peaks and valleys on the graph, especially in what is supposed to be humor. If we could only remove the valleys!" "The program is used purely as a vehicle. Never mind discriminating audiences. The mass counts. No representation for the minority!" "We're giving people what they want. But the 4½ billion dollar tab is picked up by the advertiser, and passed on to the consumer. It has been established that white women, age 18 to 49, are paramount as buyers of products. So slant it their way!" "Social responsibility? The law that speaks of the public interest? People should make their voices heard. How often do they do it?"

Coming down specifically to the influence that TV and radio exert on the language, we may refer incidentally to small bloopers or slips of the tongue that occur even with our best-known figures. Back in the days of radio, Lowell Thomas drew big laughs when he renamed Sir Stafford Cripps of the British cabinet "Sir Stifford Crapps." Was this deliberate or accidental? We never found out. More recently, Walter Cronkite in his newscast of July 16, 1974, came out with "Makarios extolled the Cypriotes to resist" (of course, he meant "exhorted"). Peter Marshall, the ultra-simpático host of "Hollywood Squares," uttered in his July 29, 1976, program the phrase "it can manifold itself in your health" (no doubt he meant "manifest"). Another of my favorite newscasters, Rolland Smith of CBS-TV, came out with "gives credit to seasonable factors" (it was obvious that he meant "seasonal"). Still another described Mikhail Baryshnikov of ballet fame as "a Russian ex-patriot," for "expatriate"—deliberate, perhaps?

Was it creativeness that led John Camper to say, "when he 'lucked' it into his first acting job"? Or May Moore to offer, "You don't know your elbow from your end zone!"? Or Johnny Carson, in his September 13, 1977, program, to coin (deliberately) an imaginary singular from an equally imaginary plural: "How does it feel to get one applau?" But for this he had historical precedent. After the Norman Conquest, the English, hearing the Norman-Picard French *cherise* (modern French *cerise*), were misled by the final -s sound into thinking it was a plural, and appropriated the word as "cherries"; they then coined "cherry" for its singular.

A WQXR newscaster says: "The police made a positive identity of the victim" (for "identification"). The Croatian Nationalist hijacking of a plane, attended by a bomb explosion and the death of a bomb squad member, led to a revelation of ignorance on the part of two separate newscasters, one of whom made "Croatian" rhyme with "Laotian," while the other made "Croat" rhyme with "goat." There was also "We avoid accidents from happening," but this was from an invited bureaucrat who was being interviewed.

The written caption for CBS-TV's October 31, 1975, newscast bore the legend "homocide" for "homicide." Whether this was due to ignorance of spelling and etymology, reflection of sloppy pronunciation, or analogical pull from "homosexual," we do not know. Sloppy pronunciation was involved in the original theme song for "All in the Family," where the next to the last line sounded like "Gee, our roller sour great!" This so puzzled me that I wrote to the program and requested them to clear it up. They replied that it was meant to be "Gee, our old La Salle ran great!" Not only did this make sense, but when the new series came out, the theme song was retaken and made to sound understandable.

One weasely feature appears in the pronunciation of "cellulite" (a made-up word that does not yet appear in the dictionaries) as "cell-u-leet." This is on a par with "mid-wiff-er-y" for "midwifery," and is a sample of "precious" pronunciations designed to impress the victims of advertising.

Jean Stafford, in *The New York Times* (September 15, 1974) accuses TV of "Murdering the English Language." Strong words, but the writer cites chapter and verse: Cronkite asks us to "declare a honeymoon." How do you declare a honeymoon, when you have to attend the funerals of so many decent, law-abiding words, asks Ms. Stafford. There are many samples of excessive functional change ("to alibi," "to structure," "a conceptual construct," "a meaningful rethink"). There are pronunciations like Eisenhower's "nucular" and Kennedy's "Cubar" (but can you blame TV for recording and reporting the way Presidents speak?). Cronkite's own "maras-chee-no," "licorish," and "Febuary" (in the last of which he is joined by Mary McLoughlin, also of CBS) would have been more to the point, as also Garner Ted Armstrong's (he is normally not only a fine speaker, but an able writer) "infectuous" for "infectious" and "prodigial" for "prodigal." "All aspirin is not alike," "feeling nauseous," "gasid indigestion," "you get a lot of clean with Tide" come in for a drubbing; but they pertain to commercial advertising rather than to the "pure" language of TV. "Opt for," "life-styles," "living situations," "career experiences" are other stylistic gems. From the language of politics, faithfully reproduced on TV, come such jewels as a congressman's pronunciation of "accelerate" with the first syllable pronounced "ass-"; the same Solon goes on to defend "the actions of he and his associates, which, militarily speaking, showed maximum patriotism under the mandate of his command." Then there is Jeb Magruder's reply "We was us" to Senator Ervin's inquiry "Who were 'we'?" Ms. Stafford's conclusion is that in the mental disorder of the TV networks, "the lazy, wool-gathering tongue stupefies the brain."

Another writer, commenting in verse on the previous article, mentions all his pet peeves, which turn out to be popular clichés: "putting it all together," "you name it," "no way," "viable," "you know," "you'd better believe."

A final, international note of criticism was voiced by Mike Royko in commenting on a TV show that purported to be about a Polish-American family, "The Kovacks." Why, inquired Mr. Royko, were these Poles given a Hungarian name? Why was the accompanying music either Russian Gypsy or Hungarian Gypsy? Why did Mrs. Kovack wear a Russian babushka? ¿Quién sabe? At any rate, the correct Hungarian spelling for that name is Kovács, not Kovack.

Another international note was struck by Johnny Carson in his discussion of the televised version of *The Godfather* (November 12, 1977), when the name of Corleone was transformed into *"Coglioni"* (an obscene word in Italian). But he may have gotten this from the film itself, where an ignorant Italian-American character pronounces it that way.

What of linguistic creativity on the part of, or in connection with, radio-TV? "Electronic press" for TV newscasts has been mentioned; it first came to my notice in a *New York Times* article by John O'Connor. In the same article, Barbara Walters was described as "a million-dollar baby in a five-and-ten cent store."

"Talking heads" is TV parlance for a program showing prominent people saying something intellectual, rather than offering action shots of them getting on and off planes and uttering appropriate platitudes. There is "dreck," a term equivalent to "baloney" fed to viewers who are not too bright. In connection with a discussion of group names for animals ("a pride of lions," "a covey of quail," etc.), Tony Randall and Johnny Carson apparently improvised humorous terms, such as "a ham of actors" and "a shtick of comedians." On "The Jeffersons," the expression "dinch" was coined, on the analogy of "brunch," to be used if you get up in the afternoon. Newscaster Connie Chung seems responsible for "busy jewelry." "Sweathogs" is the inelegant name created for "slow learners" on "Welcome Back, Kotter!" Quite anonymous is the sarcastic "dim viewer" to signify a TV viewer who takes a dim view of what he is forced to view.

Going back to the days of radio, Jack Anderson, commemorating Walter Winchell, reminds us that he coined such terms as "souse-iety," "debutramp," "playbore," "swelegant," "Chicagorilla," along with a timely prophecy on the eve of World War II: "Britain will marry Hitler in the fall; the marriage will blow up in a world war."

⑥ Radio's CB Language

Radio alone is responsible for the new language of the new trucking subculture, which has now spread to the so-called Citizens' Radio Bands, whereby any two vehicles can communicate. TV has helped to publicize it, but not to the same extent as the press.

Originally a secret language, like the argot or *jobelyn* of the thieves who collaborated with François Villon, or the rhyming tongue of the English Cockneys, it bears the stigma of weaselism, as something designed to confuse and befuddle the uninitiate. But this characteristic was soon lost. Its use became generalized, and was ultimately codified in article, pamphlet, and book form, so that it became accessible to all CB set users, as well as to their antagonists, the state troopers assigned to control traffic along the nation's highways. But its picturesque features endure, and the "language" itself, like the "bubble and squeak" of London's East End, seems destined for a long life. An entire best-selling volume has been cooked up from this new, strange tongue.

Many of the terms are designed to warn drivers of the location and activities of speed-law enforcers. "Smokey," "Bear," or "Smokey Bear" can be any law-enforcement officer, but more specifically a state trooper. "Smokey taking pictures" is police radar. "Smokey on the ground" is a trooper out of his patrol car, while "Smokey on rubber" is the trooper in his patrol car. "Bear in the air" is a police helicopter. "Tijuana taxi" denotes a police car with lights and insignia, but "plain brown wrapper" is an unmarked police car. "Bubble gum machine" is a police emergency light. "To feed the bears" is to get a ticket. "County mountie" is a local sheriff, while "boy scouts" are the state police, and "local yokel" is a city police officer. Police headquarters becomes "the zoo," or "the bear cave."

But there are occasions when outside help of one sort or another is needed, even by CBers. Then any police officer becomes "the man in blue," while a fireman is "the man in slicker," and a doctor or ambulance attendant is "the man in white." The ambulance itself is "bone box," and a wrecker is "dragging wagon."

The CBers' secondary worry after the police is the FCC (Federal Communications Commission), which controls, at least in theory, the use and volume of bands, and is affectionately known as "Uncle Charlie" or "Daddy-O"; but "panic in the streets" means that the FCC is monitoring the area. "Glory card" is an FCC license.

There are cute place-name designations. "Bikini State" is Florida. "Big A" is Atlanta. "Music Town" is Nashville. "Choo-Choo Town" is Chattanooga. "Flag Town" is Washington, D.C., while "Shaky Town" is San Francisco (could this be a reminder of the great earthquake?). There is even, for the edification of the underprivileged Northeast, "The Dirty Side" for New York and New Jersey.

There are picturesque expressions for the gentler sex. "XYL" designates a wife (ex-young lady), while "YL" alone stands for girl friend. Since CBers believe in equality, "XYM" (ex-young man) stands for husband. "Seat covers" are company, usually female, in the vehicle. "Check the seat covers" means "Don't miss the female passenger in that car; her skirt is pulled up." "Pavement princess" is a roadside prostitute, but "go-go girls," which sounds sexy, is used for a traveling consignment of hogs. "Eights" are kisses; "threes and eights" means so long and kisses.

For themselves, when organized into a club, CBers have devised "chain gang"; "ears" is a CB radio or antenna, but "ballet dancer" is an antenna that is not properly tied down. "Blessed event" is a new CB set. Instead of the customary "wow!" as an all-purpose exclamation, many CBers have gone back to a traditional and genteel "mercy!" On the other hand, they are just as apt to use the Southern "cotton-pickin' " as an all-around derogatory adjective. "Throwing carriers" means overriding other transmissions.

They are concerned with safety. A driver hauling a dangerous cargo is known as a "suicide jockey." Two sayings have sprung up: "Keep your nose between the ditches and Smokey out of your britches" ("Drive safely and look out for speed traps!") and "Keep the greasy side down and the shiny side up" ("Drive safely, and don't overturn your car!"). "Double nickels" refers to the current 55-mile-an-hour speed limit. "Blow the doors down!" is a courteous invitation to pass.

From the days when the language was a prerogative of the truckers come such terms as "chicken coop" (truck weighing station); "swindle sheet" and "comic books" (trucker's log sheets or logbook); "green stamps" (dollars for toll roads); "eat-um-up" (truck-stop café). "Pregnant roller skate" is the contemptuous term for a Volkswagen of the Beetle variety. Unexplained is the Spanish *"queso"* (cheese) for conversation.

Side by side with the full-fledged CB language, there developed a numerical system, known as the "10 Code" (10 is the first figure, and identifies the transmission as a CB product). This saves time on the air, and is not too difficult to learn. Did it originate as a copy of the frequently used police numerical code for various types of crimes ("Two-five in progress at supermarket on the corner of Fifteenth and Vermont," as often heard on

such programs as "Adam-12")? Its coded messages run all the
way from 10-1 to 10-200. Here are a few of the more familiar
ones:

10-2	"Receiving you well."
10-4	"O.K. Message received."
10-5	"Please relay message."
10-6	"Busy. Please wait."
10-9	"Please repeat."
10-11	"You're talking too fast."
10-12	"Visitors present."
10-17	"Urgent message."
10-23	"Stand by."
10-30	"Do not conform to FCC rules." (This could be dangerous.)
10-33	"Emergency! Mayday!" ("Breaker for 10-33" means "I'm breaking in on account of a very serious situation.")
10-34	"Trouble at this station. Help needed!"
10-39	"Your message delivered."
10-41	"Please tune to channel—"
10-43	"Traffic tie-up at—"
10-44	"I have a message for—"
10-73	"Speed trap at—"
10-75	"You are causing interference."
10-84	"My phone number is—"
10-85	"My address is—" (This and the preceding one could also have dangerous features.)
10-100	"Stand by; bathroom urgency." (This is described as quite informal.)
10-200	"Police needed at—"

Interestingly, the Denver police department found out
through experimentation that there are fewer mistakes and
misunderstandings on the police radio when officers communicate in English rather than in the numerical codes they use to

disguise what they're talking about. Henceforth, the Denver police will call a robbery a robbery instead of a "Ten-three-three in progress." For years they talked in code while plain citizens used plain English. Now the police revert to plain talk, while CBers use a lingo that only other CBers are supposed to understand. A curious reversal of roles.

If CB and its language have their enthusiasts, they also have their detractors, chief among them what might be described as "CB widows."

A wife complains that her once happy marriage is now a nightmare, constantly interrupted by "breakers." Her once loving husband now comes home and greets and kisses the radio instead of her and the children. There is no privacy, not even in bed: "Breaker! Breaker! You in there, Good Buddy?"

What is she to do? "If you can't lick them, join them!" will hardly work in this case, says columnist Helen Bottel.

7 The Big Guns of Media Advertising

A tout seigneur, tout honneur! First honors go by right to what is most complete, most thorough, most pervading. Printed advertising can give only a pallid replica, through photographs, of the immediate visual image brought to you by TV. TV and radio share the auditory message, often in musical form. Sponsors of nationwide fame are brought in to praise the product, whether they actually use it or not. Often the radio or TV performer also voices the commercial message, which is handled with a reverence worthy of a religious cause. To my knowledge, only one performer-producer, Alfred Hitchcock, showed, mainly by the inflection of his voice, the contempt he properly felt for "a commercial!" Only one newscaster, Long John Nebel, "The Voice of Midnight," gave out commercials as though he was really convinced as well as convincing. Programs may be omitted, replaced, cut down. Commercials very seldom are.

There is nothing haphazard about the handling of radio and TV advertising. An entire science dubiously mislabeled "demographics" has been worked out by the networks and the advertising agencies, working in close concert, with elaborate studies of audiences with regard to age, sex, spending power. Yet commercials are often linked, at least in my opinion, with the wrong programs. Why should a fictional TV offering that deals with bombings and violence be interspersed with commercials chanting the praises of detergents, floor waxes, and window polishers? The former should by rights appeal to men, the latter to women. Conversely, what links a roistering commercial about beer to a tender love story?

But worse than this, there are programs that build up tremendous suspense in the right kind of audience, a suspense that is broken, and hard to rebuild, by a commercial for paper towels. True, the break gives you a chance to get up and stretch, or visit the kitchen or toilet—breaks you don't get when the program runs on without interruption for an hour or more, as on educational channels. But is this sufficient compensation for the violent break in your sense of suspense? No researcher has yet thought of testing a selected group of viewers for adrenaline, blood pressure, and possible long-range psychological consequences under conditions of on-again-off-again viewing of exciting pictures interrupted by silly, tranquilizing commercials. The experiment might be worth trying.

Many viewers have been heard to complain about the lack of balance between the sound volume of a program that is as often as not whispered, and the accompanying loud, screeching singing commercial, which seems to have been constructed for the hard of hearing, the deaf (and dumb, in both senses of the word), or for members of the generation brought up on earsplitting rock concerts and discotheque music. The singing is often frantic and incomprehensible, and the message, for what it may be worth, is utterly lost. At times this is due to the diction rather than the volume. There is one ditty that in its TV version is properly enunciated: "The road to riches—starts at the Dime!" In the radio version, it sounds like: "The road to riches—da-da-da-da!" More detailed criticism of the singing commercials, along with their history, will appear in Chapter 8.

Of course, what we describe above does not invariably happen. There are plenty of singing commercials that can be listened to with pleasure as often as they recur; one example is "The Road to Morocco," designed to attract tourists both to the country and the airline. Other commercials have such humorous features that they can amuse you over and over again. Alka-Seltzer, with its Jewish humor stories and its British accents in describing Cookie and his meat loaf, is a perfect example. Another is the little koala bear that appears for Qantas, which it hates. A third is Robert Morley, inviting us to "Come home! All is forgiven!" Why can't the advertising agencies get wise to themselves and create schools of taste in advertising? I cheerfully acknowledge that I am influenced by my own taste in these matters. What appeals to me may not appeal to millions of others, and vice versa. Yet, in a sense, good taste, like good language, can be described as objective.

Good-looking girls in scanty attire may always be relied upon to hold the attention of male viewers, whatever they are advertising. But they usually advertise products meant to be bought by women, like cosmetics. Here it may be argued that the fifty-year-old woman on the plain side may be inspired to emulate the twenty-year-old American beauty, and think of herself as reflecting the image on the screen.

More serious is the criticism that deals with the endless, infinitely boring repetition of the same commercial episode, night after night, over all stations, particularly when the message and its actors are uninspiring (Maxwell House coffee, a paper towel that absorbs more than any other, another paper towel that weighs more than its competitors, for instance). For this abuse I suggest a remedy that most taxpayers will approve of—a federal tax on excessive repetition of any given commercial. But some advertisers do not hesitate to vary their offerings. Whatever one may think of Mr. Whipple and his squeezable toilet paper, it varies often enough to preclude nausea.

Phonetic peculiarities are sometimes artfully brought in to

lend enchantment, as in the explosive initial *b* that makes the appeal of beer, beef, and butter more appetizing. To offset this, however, Madison Avenue often devises radio and TV forms that are thoroughly revolting, like "Take a rat to lunch!," the extermination of roaches with a view of the corpses, or, in the medical field, the graphic description of sinuses or hemorrhoids ("Preparation Itch?"), or the view of a stomach in trouble from excess acidity. I thoroughly realize that certain products cannot be make to look and sound as appetizing as the tempting displays of platters of pasta with a rich tomato sauce, or of mixed salads with a lovely dressing, or of an assortment of tasty cheeses. Still, could not something be done to avoid turning the viewer's stomach?

For what concerns the health and medicine field, the *New England Journal of Medicine* calls attention to another problem by pointing out that in addition to the overnumerous medical and illness dramas, there are far too many commercials "for stomach gas, constipation, headaches, nervousness, sleeplessness, arthritis, anemia, the despair of malodorousness, sweat, yellow teeth, dandruff, boils, piles" (they forgot "the heartbreak of psoriasis"), indicating that Americans who are overconcerned with health are turned into nervous wrecks by having the finger of advertising point to all the thousands of potential danger spots in their anatomy.

Then there are commercials that are sickeningly sweet, like "He touched me!" in connection with a skin softener, or the "pure golden honey" that goes into a bread. Others are contradictory, as when a heavy, expensive automobile is described as a "land cruiser" in an advertisement that makes its appeal to the rich, as a "gas guzzler" in a commercial for another car that is small and light.

Many weasel words find their way into food advertising, "natural" and "real" among them. What are "natural" ingredients, as applied to bread, yogurt, even toothpaste? How are potato chips made "real"? Why is Coca-Cola "the real thing"? Why does the director of an advertising agency call this sort of thing "attitudinal advertising"?

Accepting the last term for what it may be worth, we find that it is highly recommended for restaurant-menu compilers. "Don't just say prunes," counsel the experts. "Label them 'spiced imperial prunes.' Not just apricots, but 'New Zealand apricots.' If the customer asks for the waiter's advice, suggest items that are ready to go, like prime ribs of beef or lasagne. If you must use French in your menus, accompany it with English translations." Good advice, and not too weasely.

Is there a way of avoiding commercial advertising on radio-TV, outside of having a remote-control attachment or control that shuts out the commercial without your having to move from your comfortable position? There is, by concentrating on municipal radio stations and educational TV channels. This, however, has its own exquisite drawbacks. Since educational channels depend upon gifts from government, foundations, and individuals, they often conduct campaigns to stimulate cash donations from their viewers. These can be overlong and extremely boresome, with many minutes devoted to phone calls to and from prospective contributors, both real and imaginary. It might be said that the commercial appeal is there, though in a noble cause.

For this, however, an explanation of sorts is forthcoming from John Jay Iselin, president of WNET-TV, and Lawrence Grossman, president of PBS. The appeal to viewers, who supply only 25 percent of operating funds, is to some extent due to the partial withdrawal of the Ford Foundation, partly to the fact that federal support is conditioned upon every federal dollar being matched by $2.50 from other sources.

Why the unbearable length of the breaks (twenty a day while the campaign is on), which run from six to eight minutes each? Because the stations have learned that as soon as the pitch ends and the programming starts up again, the authentic phone calls from outside viewers stop coming. Therefore in prime time (8:00 to 11:00 P.M.) the WNET pledge periods carry a total of forty to forty-eight minutes a night of fund-raising appeals, as compared with less than thirty minutes of commercials on the major networks. The quality of WNET programs makes this worthwhile. But intellectual appeal, too, carries its price tag.

8 Advertising Techniques and Practices

With a few praiseworthy exceptions, one of the most unpleasant features of radio-TV is the singing commercial, or jingle. Some are screeched out, usually by a mixed chorus, in such fashion as to be utterly incomprehensible to the listener. Their jarring effect is, of course, counterproductive. You usually know, in a general way, what they are advertising, and you are predisposed against it. The majority are understandable, but unpleasant, illogical, unfunny. The "Take me! I'm yours!" of an airline is typical. The request to "take me" (where I want to go) makes sense; but why am I yours? Another airline jingle, however, always hits my funny bone, for a very special reason: "We're American Airlines, doing what we do best!" There is a little French poem describing the attitude of a group of little rabbits, who declare themselves to be thoroughly indifferent to human national, international, or philosophical problems. Each stanza ends: *"Nous sommes les petits lapins—assis sur nos petits derrières"* ("We are the little rabbits—squatting on our little behinds"). The similarity in wording never fails to send me.

Children's choruses used in commercial fashion are, as a rule, among the most incomprehensible. But there is one that no one fails to get: a little group of tots chanting "Ring around the collar!" to the tune of "Ring Around the Rosie."

The musical piracies that go on in the world of commercials are fantastic, and lead one to wonder whether suitable royalties have been paid to the original composers, if alive. But alive or dead, nothing is sacred. It is not only popular songs but also operatic airs, symphonies, even religious music, like the touch of Gregorian chant that was initiated, I believe, in "Shopright knows the answer!" but is now pressed into service by several advertisers.

What connection is there between *The Bridge over the River Kwai* and a certain brand of gasoline? The use of Modugno's "Volare" is at least justified by the name of the car, and the tune is well sung by a night club star, Sergio Franchi. Rather ingenious is the commercial that flashes various appetizing foods on the screen, interspersed with occasional glimpses of a no-calorie cola drink. For all the dishes, the vocal accompaniment is "NO-NO," for the cola it is "YES-YES." This is set to various tunes, "Dixie" and "Yankee Doodle" among them.

Hamburger houses specialize in "We do it all for you!" (Really? Don't they make anything on the deal?), and "Have it your way!," for which the variant is "Hold the pickle! Hold the lettuce!," as though the consumer were physically unable to remove such unwanted constituents from his own hamburger-plus-roll.

One commercial displays such lack of good taste that it borders on lack of decency. The singing voice imitates that of Maurice Chevalier, whose memory should be respected. The pictured character is a frog, with Chevalier's straw hat and cane. He sings, in a croaking voice, a tune once dear to the heart of the singer, with a minor change in its final word: "Thank heaven for little cars!" So far, no protest from the French. They are seemingly above noticing such vulgar displays. Our advertisers should be cautioned, however, against trying something similar with the Jews, the Italians, the Irish, or the blacks. They might get an explosive reaction.

The history of commercial jingles is interesting, even if the product is not. There is a book on the subject, *Great Songs of Madison Avenue,* by Peter and Craig Norback. The first recorded jingle, for Wheaties, was introduced by General Mills in the 1920s. At that same period, Paul Hindemith invented the term *Gebrauchsmusik,* "music for use," to describe a form of composition that would be the antithesis of ivory-tower music. Hindemith's *Gebrauchsmusik* is said to survive in "You Deserve a Break Today," which sells hamburgers.

The point of jingles is the same as that of popular music: finding a "hook" that is repeated *ad nauseam,* and that the listener can't get away from, whether he likes it or not. It is estimated that in one twenty-four-hour period more people have heard the Chock Full o' Nuts jingle than have heard the Beethoven Eroica since it was composed in 1803.

Are jingles profitable to their authors? For a local or regional commercial, the going rate is between $1,000 and $2,500. If the jingle is part of a nationwide campaign, the writer may expect $20,000 to $40,000, or even more; but no royalties or residuals.

As one might expect, the competition is fierce. That kind of money is pretty good for twenty-eight seconds of music. There is a movement afoot to "unionize" jingle writers so that they may own the rights to their own music and be paid for demonstrations of their products to which they are summoned, even if their jingle is rejected.

There is an advertising technique that might be called, for want of a better name, "attraction by subtraction." This consists of advertising and selling a cheaper product (not necessarily inferior, but less expensive to produce) at a higher price than the one for which it substitutes.

The technique first came to my notice during a visit to Martha's Vineyard. I wanted to top off an Italian dinner I was preparing for my hosts with a cup of good, strong espresso coffee. None of my favorite espresso brands was available on the island at that period. But there was a possible substitute—a coffee selling for nearly twice the price of regular American brands, which featured an admixture of chicory. Chicory I knew well, having tried and liked the mixture in New Orleans, and I had even made the mixture for myself, by the simple expedient of adding some powdered chicory (at that time it sold for fifteen cents a box) to regular coffee. This particular brand, however, advertised itself extravagantly: chicory was what had traveled with Napoleon's armies and contributed to their many victories. (The advertising material carefully refrained from stating the historical truth—that the French, and indeed the entire continent of Europe—had been forced to replace coffee with chicory because of the British naval blockade, and that as soon as Napoleon fell, practically everybody went back to coffee.)

There is an interesting aftermath. Recently, during the great coffee rip-off of 1976–1977, a supermarket that shall remain unnamed posted advance warnings to its customers that prices were going to go up and up, and urged them to boycott the product. This antedated even New York Consumer Commissioner Elinor Guggenheimer's proclamation of a nationwide coffee boycott. Late in 1977, however, the same supermarket displayed on its shelves a canned one-pound coffee described as "the great New Orleans mixture of coffee and chicory," at $9.19 a pound can, roughly double the price of the most expensive brands of ordinary coffee. The manager, to whom I had suggested boxed chicory powder for individual mixing (this is available in New Orleans for less than fifty cents a six-ounce box, and could conceivably be ordered from its New Orleans producers), had said that powdered chicory could not be found by the chain's suppliers.

Since my Martha's Vineyard experience, at least twenty years ago, I have witnessed many repetitions of "attraction by subtraction," nearly always featuring a health element, real or imaginary: margarine for butter; eggs with the yolk removed; imitation sausage, ham, and bacon made out of soybeans (cholesterol, you know). A latecomer on the market is Swiss "X Beer," with the alcohol partly subtracted (remember the "needle beer" of Prohibition days, with an alcoholic content of less than 2 percent? Nobody liked it). I haven't tried buying or drinking it, but I should not be surprised to find it priced higher than full-strength imported beers. This is all part of the great modern economic process of less and less product for more and more money.

Slightly different in nature is the labeling of some domestic products by their foreign names. The French froth at the mouth when they hear of "American champagne" or "Spanish champagne." They hold that the sacred name of "champagne" should be reserved for what issues from the Champagne district of France. I have often suspected that part of the rapprochement between France and Italy after World War II is due to the fact that unlike the Americans and Spaniards, the Italians disdain to call their sparkling wines "champagne," and insist on their own native term, "spumante," even if their American advertisers mispronounce it "spumanti." But the Americans have gone one step further in their misuse of "champagne." They have dubbed something that is basically a beer "Champale."

One of the more distressing features of radio-TV advertising is the personal appearance on commercials of people of renown who push a product that they may or may not use, but that they pretend to use. Columnist Jack O'Brian, who coined the terms "videotrocities" and "commershills" for these occasions, listed a few of the emoluments paid by the advertisers to these hired performers—a cool tax-free million to Lord Olivier and almost the same amount to Gregory Peck and Steve McQueen; a quarter of a million each to Joe Namath, Bing Crosby, Ralph Bellamy, Joe DiMaggio, and Carlos Montalbán; all the way down to Pearl Bailey, whose chicken-plucking is worth $50,000. Another correspondent adds Jim Backus, Henry Fonda, and

Danny Thomas to the list, and quotes the Screen Actors' Guild to the effect that its members collected a total of $62 million in 1976 commercials. O'Brian adds the comment that every cent of this, plus the advertising agencies' fees, is paid for by the viewing public, since they are all added to the price of the advertised products. Do TV watchers realize how much they are really paying for their supposedly "free" entertainment, he wonders?

There is, in addition, an element of what might almost be described as professional prostitution in this type of advertising. Does Joe DiMaggio really use the Mr. Coffee machine? Does he really keep all his savings in the Bowery Savings Bank? Does Rocky Graziano really get his transmission fixed where he says he does, and as often?

For reasons of ethnic pride, I am personally most perturbed by the great Italian-American trio—DiMaggio, Rocky, and Joe Gorgonzola (pardon! Garagiola). The first one worries me, among other things, because of the way he pronounces his own name, with a *zh*-sound that is neither English nor Italian (Florentines alone among Italians might use it, but for a single, never a double, *g*). Rocky bothers me because of the way he murders what is meant to be a lower-class Metropolitan New York second-generation-Italian accent; I can only describe his rendering as "ineffable" (Latin-based synonym for "unspeakable"); I have often wondered what his finger-stabbing at the end of his commercial is supposed to betoken. Garagiola annoys me on general grounds; he's an expert, and a good one, in sports, but he'll sponsor anything that comes along.

There is also a confusion that is created in the minds of the viewers by the different roles assumed by these personalities. David Janssen had gained a measure of credibility as a physician in a white coat while he was recommending medical specialties; then, quite suddenly, he turned into Harry O, a private eye. Right now he is trying to get back on the gravy train as a medical expert. But his credibility is tarnished. And is Joe really Mr. Coffee or Mr. Bowery?

As a reaction to these practices, or possibly for reasons of economy, a few industrialists have chosen to appear in person. One was extremely successful as a lower-class character named Jerry, who, with an impeccable accent, advertised special sales prices "to union members and deir famblies." Unfortunately he ran afoul of some government watchdog unit or other, and was practically forced out of business. Why not go into the movies? He'd have us all in stitches.

There is the man who cackles like one of his own excellent chickens, though he has recently taken voice lessons. There is the "voice from beyond the grave" of the producer of ice cream, who is also interested in spreading his chain of franchised outlets. He recently saw the light and had himself replaced by professional actors, who actually crack jokes about getting him off the commercial. Then there is the fake (or perhaps authentic) New Englander who chants the praises of a fine bread. I have nicknamed him "Old Toothless," though he probably has more teeth than I.

Lastly, there are the native speakers who deliberately distort their own languages in an impeccably native accent. Ricardo Montalbán's *cor-DO-va* for what he knows perfectly well is *COR-do-va* goes to join Jean-Pierre Aumont's *ZEE-za-nie* for French *zee-za-NEE,* the men's cologne, and the *ca-PREE* used by a native Italian auto salesman for what he knows is *CA-pri.* And what of *Hof-brow* and *Lowen-brow* for *Hofbräu* and *Löwenbräu?* Of course, they are deferring to the ignorant habits of American speakers, who happen to be the sales targets. May their fellow-countrymen forgive them!

It is interesting to watch how techniques change. There was a time when any mention of a competing brand was utterly taboo. In fact, "brand X" was devised as a catchall to refer to any and all competitors. Perhaps there was some fear that the brand labeled and pictured as inferior might react with a lawsuit.

If this was the explanation, the legal aspect must have been definitely cleared, because in the more recent past copious reference has been made, not only by name but by actually displaying the "other" product—sometimes half a dozen "other" products at once, as in the case of an underarm antiperspirant; sometimes only two or three, as in the case of aspirin, Anacin, Bufferin, Excedrin.

One of the early instances to come to my notice was the spoken "Watch out, McDonald!" used by a competing hamburger house. At present we have Ronzoni conclusively proving, by pouring the two sauces out of their cans into a sieve, that its sauce has more firm tomato meat than Ragù's. Louis Sherry ice cream, by a similar test (slicing the container down the middle so as to expose a cross section of its contents), reveals more fruit and nuts than Breyer's (it might be objected that by the same token it has less ice cream). Those two ancient rivals, Coca-Cola and Pepsi-Cola, test each other out by a blindfold test of supposedly innocent and impartial consumers. So do Schmidts and Coors beers.

All this might be slightly more credible if the testing were conducted by a board of impartial and incorruptible arbiters. This in practice never happens, and the firm that pays for the commercial never fails to win. A weasely system, to be viewed with suspicion by the millions of viewers? Such would be my impression. To the objection "Who would pay for a neutral panel of judges and subjects?" there is a ready answer. Let the competing firms get together and share the costs. In other words, let them put their money (our money, to be more precise) where their mouths are.

In this connection, a study conducted by Ogilvy & Mather, an advertising agency, and Evaluative Criteria, Inc., a research organization, brings to light the somewhat startling fact that "comparative advertising" produces little advantage to the consumer, the advertiser, or the advertising agency; the only one who seems to benefit is the competitor whose product is being disparaged. *Media Industry Newsletter* reports: "Results indicate that comparative commercials are less believable than non-comparative ones. They create great sponsor misidentification, and they fail to prove more persuasive than non-comparative versions." A case of being hoist by one's own petard?

A related question is that of full disclosure in advertisements. Should a firm that advertises a low caloric content for its product mention the fact that it also has a high cholesterol content, owing to the presence of cocoa butter? Should the limitations of the product appear in the advertising, for, say, a magnifying glass that "helps the eyesight," but is no real substitute for prescription glasses? Someday, somewhere, there may come a ruling.

9 Advertising Clichés and Other Crimes

A good deal of language comes in clichés, meaningful only to the natives. These are stereotyped expressions that gain popularity, and are used by some sparingly, by others on every possible occasion. Some originate with radio-TV, the majority do not; but the latter are utilized to the full on radio-TV. Take, for instance, "You gotta believe!," taken over, stock, lock, and barrel, by an airline. Or the "How's your love life?" of a breath sweetener, to which the demure response of the ingenue who is posing as a tennis champion is "What's a love life?" (I would prefer "Dun't esk!"). Another airline features "Save a bundle!" An automobile ad encourages criminal tendencies (as though there weren't enough) by concluding its sales pitch with the words: "And if you're going in for a life of crime—remember —XX is a great getaway car!"

Nothing pleases the advertising agencies so much as creating their own clichés, in the hope that they may become part of the standard colloquial, and gain the force of adages; witness "Have a Pepsi Day!"; "Thanks! I needed that!"; "When [a brokerage house] speaks, people listen!"; "Thank you, [another brokerage house]!"; "[a third brokerage house] is bullish on America!"

Inventiveness is not lacking in TV advertising: "The Save Your Life Diet," "The Total Woman," "Total Fitness" (but these may have been borrowed from book titles); the "Price and Pride" slogan of one of our greatest food chains (I would parody this into "Price and Pride wait for no man!"). But the best creation, though it does play havoc with the language, comes from KLM Royal Dutch Airlines: "We'll cheerful you, and tulip you, and canal you, and cheese you, and windmill you, and give you an Amsterdam good time!" (stress on the *-dam,* for the benefit of those who enjoy mild profanity; they didn't dare use *Rotter*dam).

Erma Bombeck, in one of her inimitable columns, comes out with a list of advertised detergents, real and fancied: "All New Scum Fighter," "Power Booster," "HMQ," "All Modern," "Ultimate Perfection," to which, for good measure, she adds a list of appropriate adjectives: "advanced," "revolutionary clean," "reborn," "perfected," "renovated," "futurized," "upgraded," "reinforced," "renewed," "revised and enriched."

There is also what one might call "attraction by negation," but with positive expectations, like the name "Marty's Bum Steer" for what is, by all accounts, an excellent steak house.

There are other ingenious linguistic creations, like the "Wessonality" that is imparted to fried chicken by a cooking oil, "fleafestation" for your pets, "Schweppervescence" for a carbonated drink (but there was an earlier "Evervess," the name of a competing soda water). There is also the publicitarian description "uniquity" as a characteristic of New York City (combination of "unique" and "iniquity," with all the glamour of the two words?); as well as the "paperalysis" appearing in a magazine ad for an "automatic collator" or "foil plate," whatever that may be.

On the other hand, the most overworked words of advertising are plain and simple, like "just" and "only": "Just send in $29.50"; "You can have it for only $5.95." They have been known to backfire through misplacement, as when the ad came out "Only two pairs for $22." The astronaut's "A-OK" has been kidnapped by a laxative, which has rechristened it "M-OK."

Direct crimes against the language abound, in all divisions. There are misspellings, like "diper rash," or "How do you spell relief? R-O-L-A-I-D-S!" (The viewer may be tempted to say "I spell it C-L-I-C-K" as he switches.) With this goes "And America spells cheese K-R-A-F-T!" (What? Does no one else make cheese in America?) There are misuses of words, like "nauseous" for "nauseated" (does the man who says he's nauseous realize that he is describing himself as disgusting?); or "big, fat, beautiful hair" and "Your hair gets fat" (does the attractive blonde who presents the product mean "glossy" or "thick"?). There are combinations of the type of "gasid indigestion."

But what really hurts is the way the process of functional change (using one part of speech in the function of another), to which English unfortunately lends itself more than any other major language, with the possible exception of Chinese, is put to work: "You get a lot of *clean* with Tide"; "*Bond* the dentures to the gums"; "Have a *funner* summer" (not a misprint for "funnier," but the new comparative of the new use of "fun" as an adjective, as in "a fun party," "a fun fur." There is the candy bar that is said to be "thickerer."

The syntax, too, is sinned against: "Made for each other, like you and I"; or the jingle "Look down the street! It comes a great new car!," which sounds like a literal translation from the German unless you intersperse it with a punctuation that the tune can't carry ("It comes! A great new car!"). There is "Does everybody want Sanka?" "We do!" "So do we do!" There is "Savings banks are for people! I'm a people!," with appropriate angelic music from on high.

There are crimes against logic, like "Our tire stops 20 percent quicker!" (quicker than what?); or "Economy doesn't have to be dull!" (perhaps they meant economics?).

Best of all in this division is the "Fly me!" uttered by an attractive airline stewardess, now discontinued because someone thought he discovered an obscene connotation. Grammatically (and logically) you don't fly someone, save in the sense of "The pilot flew him to Havana," in which case the object is the passive recipient of the action, and the subject is the person who guides the plane. Quite correctly, the flight attendants' union proclaimed that its members are messengers of mercy, not geisha girls. But even if they were, "Fly with me" would be more appropriate.

Seemingly cashing in on a popular book-movie title is "Roots" Clothiers of Summit, New Jersey. Interestingly, however, not a single black appears in the brochure illustrations.

Above, I have listed a very few of the many and horrible crimes perpetrated by commercial weasel-word users against foreign languages. Conversely, one is left wondering why a word is given a foreign form when the native equivalent is available. Why "le car" instead of "the car"? Why the rare variant "Scirocco," borrowed from Italian, instead of the more common "sirocco"? Perhaps because the Italian comes closer to the Arabic original *(sharq)* for the hot south wind that blows in from the desert?

Geographical as well as linguistic misinformation abounds. Miss Universe, who was first Miss Finland, is sponsored by Finnair to participate in the following interchange: "Where is Finland?" "Finland is in Scandinavia, as everybody knows." Everybody doesn't know it, because Finland is neither geographically nor linguistically part of Scandinavia, with which it has only a cultural link due to its long association with Sweden. But the Scandinavians have no care about either their geography or their language. Their own TV ad features: "Instead of going to Europe, come to Scandinavia and schmorgasbord." For the first time, we learn that Scandinavia does not consider itself a part of Europe, and that to please American mispronouncers it puts a *sh*-sound before the *m* to describe its delicious *smörgåsbord*. (Readers are hereby reminded that High German and Yiddish are the only Germanic languages to have an initial *shm-* sound

[*Schmidt, schmalz, shmo, schmerz,* etc.]. English, Dutch, Low German, and all the *real* Scandinavian languages [Swedish, Norwegian, Danish, Icelandic] use *sm-*).

Everybody deplores excessive advertising and excessive money spent on it. Yet 1976 was the strongest year advertising has had for nearly thirty years, and the prediction for the future is for bigger and better additions to both advertising and expenditure. Advertising revenue in 1976 totaled some $33 billion, up 16.7 percent from 1975, with the greatest gains in network and local TV, where broadcast ad rates went up more than 20 percent. The growth in advertising far outstrips the growth in Gross National Product. It applies to both rates and volume.

All this is fine for a booming economy. But viewers and readers of advertising should again be reminded that they get the tab for what they view and read. Advertising is a legitimate part of the cost of doing business, and as such is generally fully deductible from corporate taxes. This is made up for by the individual taxpayer. Where not fully deductible, it is simply added to the price of the product advertised, thus going to feed the inflationary furnace that threatens to consume us all.

Should some measure of restraint be put on advertising? Figure it out for yourself. All I have endeavored to accomplish here is to prove that both the process and the language of advertising are basically weasely.

10 The Hollywood Connection

The intimate link between TV and legitimate movies needs no stressing. The latter regularly get into TV schedules, particularly for lesser, local stations, and are therefore abridged to fit a TV schedule, and copiously interlarded with commercials. TV, on the other hand, often produces its own movies, which may or may not get into movie theaters. These are usually up-to-date in content and style (for better or for worse), and produced with a view to their television use, which means that they are not axed down to the point of being made unintelligible. Also, the commercial slots are better placed, so as not to interfere too much with the action.

There was a point in movie history when the big producing studios despaired of being able to meet the relentless competition of TV, with its deceptive "for-free" feature and its evident greater comfort to the viewer. Accordingly, some studios gave up all or most of their gigantic activities, and a number of movie houses across the land closed down. Then it began to be noticed that in spite of TV there was still a sizable demand for the original Hollywood product, shorn of costly spectaculars, big historical films with rousing battle scenes and thousands of extras, and lavish musical comedies. There set in a definite trend in the direction of risqué and even pornographic pictures, at

y produced abroad, that could not be shown on TV
enalty of losing one's channel privileges. There were
ror films, dealing with bloodshed, violence, natural and
natural disasters, that could not be shown on TV because
o_ _e children who would view them and get either ideas or
nightmares. ("Cinematic neurosis" is what the psychologists call
the latter; they include symptoms of anxiety, helplessness,
sleeplessness, chest pains, breathing difficulties.)

Many of the TV prohibitions were ultimately relaxed, with
the phony expedient of a "family viewing period" (7:00 to 9:00
or 8:00 to 10:00 P.M., after which time the kiddies were supposed to have gone to bed, which they usually failed to do). But
by this time a new movie and movie theater industry had been
created. It now thrives and flourishes side by side with TV, the
new titan that has grown to the point of dwarfing its sire.

Broadly speaking, the contemporary movie industry is subject to the same strictures as its televised offspring. Before describing and exemplifying them in detail, it may be worthwhile
to mention a few linguistic creations that seem to be peculiar
to the new movies and their showplaces, and that may be
classed as weasel words only to the extent that their creation
and use indicate a modest and fairly legitimate desire for publicity. They have not yet made the dictionaries, even those of
slang.

There is, for instance, the use of "hard-top," once restricted
to a type of automobile, to distinguish a movie theater, where
the spectator is sheltered by a roof, from the open-air variety,
where he sits in his car with his best girl (more individual privacy is to be had in the latter, of course). There is a new use of
"beard" in Hollywood to describe a friend who acts as a front
for a married man who is romancing a young girl, and escorts
the man's legitimate wife around, so that she may be the last
one to know what her husband is up to. Here the earlier slang
use was to betoken an egghead, an intellectual, usually with

leftist leanings. In medieval times (and this usage survives in some northern Italian dialects), "beard" *(barba)* was applied to an uncle who took over as the natural protector of a nephew or niece if the father died or was not available; could this be the origin of the Hollywood usage?

"Four-walling" is the practice of forcing a theater or theater chain to accept one or more old or new movies in order to get the movies they want. This parallels the publishing industry's "penalty book," which the publisher accepts as a package deal from an author from whom it wants a different book.

There is a use of a French word and a coined derivative ("the *auteur* syndrome," an *"auteuristic"* filmmaker"), offered without explanation by columnist Jack O'Brian. The term seems to mean that a producer-writer writes, produces, directs, and takes all critical praise or blame for a film; Charlie Chaplin and Leo McCarey are offered as earlier examples.

Some creative ingenuity is occasionally displayed in film titles. John Wayne's *The Shootist,* for example, is not sanctioned by the dictionaries. O'Brian coins "Hawaii-Sex-O" to label what he otherwise describes as a "homo-flick," a picture dealing with homosexuality in Hawaii. Some years ago, a spectacular Italian documentary, horrible in spots, was presented under its original title, *Mondo Cane,* more recently translated by M. Trasho as "Dog of a World" (a less literal and more semantically appropriate translation would be "What a Lousy World!").

Columnist Roger Harris offers an intriguing distinction between two types of movies: "country movies" and "city movies." Country movies, which are not necessarily about the country, stress the old-time country virtues in an old-fashioned country way: you are never left in doubt as to who are the "good guys" or the "bad guys," and both always get their just deserts (he spells it "desserts," but no matter). Life is black and white, even if the picture is in color. In contrast, city movies, which are not necessarily about a city, always present problems for the viewers. If, as is not invariably the case, the bad guys get what's coming to them, were they really that bad? No redeeming features? Were the good guys really good, or just priggish? The color, even in a color movie, is always in different shades of gray.

In this connection, Vincent Canby reports the use of "accessible" as a critics' term for a film that makes sense instead of leaving you guessing, as so many city movies do.

Almost all foreign movies are city movies, though that is changing. Almost all Westerns used to be country movies, but that is changing, too. Movies like James Bond features and *Star Wars* are full of "country" heroics; but their tongue-in-cheek characteristics belie that interpretation. Sports movies are almost always country movies. But *Rocky* is a city movie. Maybe so, maybe so!

Coming down to the truly objectionable in movies, O'Brian again leads the way by collating an impressive list of box-office hosannahs for pictures, culled mainly from the pages of *Variety:* "great," "socko," "lusty," "torrid," "zingy," "wow," "smash," "hot," "soars," "booming," and similar barkable semantics. A later list, compiled by another *Variety* researcher, adds "sharp," "tall," "rich," "boffo," "tidy," "big," "fat." Vincent Canby of *The New York Times* presents a more refined list of words, along with a resolution to avoid them as much as possible in his future film reviews: "fine," "superb," "context," "narrative," "splendid," "junk," "funky," "flaky," "to dump on," "to trash," "persona," "life-style."

Elsewhere it is remarked that, once upon a time, movie myths were created by accident or ignorance. Entire research staffs devoted their time and efforts to screening out such things as historical inaccuracies or anachronisms. Today they are the result of deliberate intent, as when a "Mrs. Perdicaris" is created out of whole cloth to replace the male American citizen of Levantine origin whose kidnapping and holding for ransom in Morocco by the Rif bandit chief Raisuli led Theodore Roosevelt to issue his famous ultimatum "Perdicaris alive, or Raisuli dead!" (No, dear viewers, the Marines did *not* land in Morocco on that occasion and fight the Rifs. Perdicaris was voluntarily surrendered. And love interest was completely absent from the historical episode.) *The Wind and the Lion,* incidentally, might have been a perfect propaganda picture for the Soviets to import and display in their theaters as an example of American imperialism, save for the fact that not even the Russians would believe in its authenticity. But perhaps they might have believed that the CIA was there even in the days of Theodore Roosevelt.

The charges of excessive violence and sex leveled at TV are equally leveled at the movies. The content of 424 films rated by the Motion Picture Association of America ranged from filthy language to outright filthy acts (rated PG to X), while a mere 62 won decent straight Gs, 214 got Rs, 60 won Xs, and 150 got PGs by reason of bad language. Yet most people think PG means the film is OK.

Survive, with its cannibalism, promoted from movie theaters to TV, outrated its Nielsen time-slot competitors in New York, Los Angeles, and Chicago by more than two to one. The question was asked of *Parade:* "Why can't Hollywood produce more meaningful films these days, without sex or violence, that will entertain, educate, and emotionally involve viewers, and that won't insult the audience's intelligence?" The succinct and truthful reply: "They don't sell."

There are what Marilyn Beck, the TV figure, calls "Filmland Turkeys of the Year." Her choices for 1976–1977 include *Logan's Run, Gumball Rally, Norman, Is That You?, Missouri Breaks,* and *Lipstick* (the last, which she describes as the "first major contemporary screen treatment on the subject of rape," she calls "an outrageous violation of good taste"). The choices of her readers include "Holmes and Yo Yo," "Baretta," and "Charlie's Angels." But it is obvious that the readers threw TV original offerings into the competition.

There are serious objections concerning the purely technical devices employed in filmmaking that deserve a hearing and an airing. Taking as his text the "overblown and vastly overpraised 'Nashville,' " novelist John Malone scores the deliberate use of the sound track to prevent you from hearing what the characters are saying, with several people talking at once and background sounds drowning out the voices of the actors, or crucial conversational exchanges being whispered just beyond hearing range. He goes on to attack *M*A*S*H,* where against deafening background noises names, jokes, and insults fly back and forth too fast to follow.

"That's the way things happen in real life" is the excuse, and it is all too true. But it is also true that movies are supposed to be a form of entertainment, not of exercise in straining your ears. My own experience is that I am far too often annoyed both at the background noises (surf, traffic, machinery, rumble of train wheels) and at the loud music that most directors think is needed for the proper enjoyment of almost any picture, when silence would be ever so much more relaxing and effective. Perhaps our film industry should take some lessons in subdued and subordinate sound from Muzak.

Another legitimate complaint deals with sequels and their titles *(Godfather II, Jaws II,* etc.; this sort of thing, however, goes back all the way to *Son of the Sheik).* It has led to all kinds of lampooning. *Night Porter,* for instance, was rechristened "Next Tango in Vienna," by a European critic who noticed that *Night Porter* did for strawberry jam what *Last Tango in Paris* did for butter.

But it is not all pure lampooning. Successful films lend themselves to what might be termed "title plagiarism," if there were such a thing (no copyright on titles, as you know). A film about a black hairdresser originally scheduled to appear as "Jonathan" became *Black Shampoo* when the grosses on *Shampoo* were revealed. *Jaws* has already spawned *Deep Jaws;* here we seem to have a crossing (double-crossing, if you'll pardon the pun) with *Deep Throat,* justified by the fact that *Deep Jaws* has a pornographic angle.

As for the original *Jaws,* which has already topped *Godfather, Sound of Music, Gone with the Wind, The Sting, The Exorcist,* and *Love Story* in earnings, we have a success story based on unrelenting publicity, mainly on TV, plus the right kind of timing to coincide with the appearance of the paperback, plus a bandwagon spirit among normally discerning critics, adding up to what Stephen Farber calls "manipulative contempt for the public," a public that includes far more than the people who ordinarily get their kicks from watching dismemberments and mutilations.

One of the side effects of *Jaws* is the healthy, or perhaps unhealthy, fear of sharks it has generated in swimmers and bathers, to the point where CBS coined the expression *"Jaws-*omania," or "fear of sharks" (*"Jaws-*ophobia" would have been more accurate).

Another columnist wonders why sharks should have such a bad reputation. Yet terms like "loan shark" and "pool shark" antedate *Jaws.* Is it possible that sharks have at least in part earned their reputation?

So, by the way, have modern movies.

The Arts, Performing and Otherwise

There is no need to stress the link between the radio-TV complex and those forms of entertainment that antedate modern mechanization. The legitimate theater, the stage spectacle in musical or dancing form (opera, operetta, concert, vocal or instrumental solo performance, symphony, ballet, and other forms of the dance), preceded in part even that other great medium of information and propaganda, the press. They share with the media the characteristic of publicity, which lends itself to weasely treatment. To a lesser degree, the publicitarian feature extends even to nonperforming branches of the arts: painting, sculpture, architecture.

In a lengthy article that appeared in the Arts and Leisure section of *The New York Times* (August 29, 1976), Clive Barnes gathered under one roof the opinions of a group of outstanding experts in the various artistic fields concerning the present and future status of their various specialties in connection with the American scene. He prefaced their remarks with some considerations of his own. The all-pervading concern with governmental and public subsidies, he thought, branded the performing arts as basically elitist, hence not in accord with the uncompromisingly democratic American tradition. "While the arts may be for all the people, not all the people are for the arts," he concluded, going on to point to the danger that government funding for the arts might become a political football, with knitting bees and other "folk arts" taking precedence over true cultural values. Robert Brustein, dean of the Yale Drama School, reinforces this thesis when he contrasts genuine artistic experience with "cocktail party chitchat, Kulchur [sic], or mindless diversion."

Yet the clamor for government support will not be stilled. Julius Rudel, artistic director of the New York City Opera, boldly demands both subsidy and elitism. "Art is not and never has been for everyone; it is for an elite," he pronounces; yet "an elite already exists, ready for discovery, in every class, race, religion, ethnic group, and even sex." But even he has to admit that a congressman once referred to the projected Kennedy Center for the Performing Arts as "a pleasure palace on the Potomac for toe and belly dancing."

Government-funded or not, there is a consensus of guarded optimism for the future of the arts, voiced by Beverly Sills (self-declared "the Beatles of the Opera") for music and opera; by Alexander Cohen, Joseph Papp, and Tammy Grimes for the stage; by Thomas Hoving of New York's Metropolitan Museum for painting and sculpture (but Robert Motherwell thunders out against "anti-painting," which he defines as exhibitionism, self-mutilation, terrorism concepts of art instead of art itself; included are cartoons, painted photographs, graffiti, and other assorted horrors).

The greatest enthusiasm is displayed for ballet and other forms of the dance by spokespeople such as Martha Graham, Lincoln Kirstein, and Lucia Chase. Kirstein goes so far as to describe the present condition of the dance in the United States as "probably better than anywhere else in the world," the Bolshoi notwithstanding.

Interestingly, screen and TV were included in Barnes's study of the arts. Here the picture is not so bright. Norman Lear deplores the fact that the average viewer spends six hours a day watching TV, having turned inward rather than outward because of lack of inspiration from our political leadership. Evidently, what is good for Norman Lear is not good for the nation, and he is man enough to admit it. Speaking for Hollywood, Peter Bogdanovich hails the current "complete freedom from censorship" (this causes Barnes to wonder whether the demands of the box office do not constitute the ultimate in censorship). But Bogdanovich himself deplores lack of taste and too many sequels, like "Godson Part 6" and "Son of Jaws." Another filmmaker, Eleanor Perry, adds the comment that the movies should feature less greed for profit and fewer Halloween tricks and play more on true human emotions; but this demands "creativity, imagination, ability, originality, talent; in short," she ruefully concludes, "a hopeless suggestion."

Linguistic creations in the artistic field abound. Not all qualify as weasel words or expressions, curious though they may be. From the theater comes a novelty, "sheltered production," which is defined as trying out a play or musical in a small locale, with a limited audience, for as many as a dozen performances before the production is finally and officially launched; the advantage is said to be that snags can be unsnagged and last-minute changes made before the general public is let in on the secret. "Gypsies" are described as hoofers who try out for a chorus line. A "signature" is a singer's theme song, the piece for which he or she is best known and most applauded. For Ella Fitzgerald, for instance, it's "A Tisket a Tasket"; but it changes from country to country. In Germany, they prefer her singing "Mack the Knife"; in Italy, "How High the Moon"; in England, "Every Time We Say Good-Bye"; in France, "Mr. Paganini," which in the United States is Martha Raye's signature. The Italians call this sort of thing a singer's *cavallo di battaglia,* "battle horse." *Prima donna assoluta,* an extravagant term (what can be more absolute than first?), though Italian in form, seems to be an American coinage of publicitarian (therefore weasely) intent.

"Pilobolus" is the imaginative name of a new type of ballet and the group that practices it, featuring dancers in a cell-like cluster, bending outward with great vitality. The name is borrowed from a fungus that seeks the light by bending and twisting toward it as it grows, finally exploding with tremendous energy and shooting out its spores.

On the jocular side are "kidvid," for a children's program, as in "A Saturday Kidvid Ghetto"; and Jim Stafford's "hickie," a cross between "hick" and "hippie," applied to dwellers in the Florida swamps. Then there is the "family breadloser," a term applied to Pippin, who plays the horses in his spare time. O'-Brian paid a visit to Sir Lew Grade (someone called him "Sir Low Grade," but that is obviously a misnomer) and was placed with his wife and daughters in the royal box at the theater; he couldn't refrain from calling it "the Royal Loo" (a loo pun). London's Tate Art Gallery was criticized for spending too much of the taxpayers' money on a blue plaque with the words "Starlit Waters" painted on it in green, one foot high, with an orange fishnet draped over it; a columnist couldn't resist the temptation to label this news item "In Poor Tate?" "New Brutalism" was applied to a style of architecture for airports said to be "sociofugal" rather than "sociopetal," whatever those terms may mean.

Some more serious criticisms are advanced against the handling of the performing arts. One correspondent complains about a Broadway play and a contemporaneous movie sketch of the late 1930s, laid in New Amsterdam before the coming of the English, in both of which productions the younger actors spoke a perfect English, but the older ones spoke with a pronounced Dutch accent. This reflected the language situation in millions of immigrant families in the 1930s, but hardly that of New Amsterdam in the 1600s. But if the movies and TV can indulge in historical inaccuracies and anachronisms, why not the stage?

The recent revival of Scott Joplin has brought to light, among other items of interest, that as late as 1912 the word "jazz" was in such dirty disrepute that when La Rocca's Original Dixieland Jazz Band was organized, the word was tidied up and spelled "jass." (Joplin's real contribution was jazz's predecessor, ragtime.) The etymology of "jazz" is still very much in dispute. One possibility that seems to have been overlooked is French semi-slang *jaser*, "to chatter, to talk volubly and idly"; but the etymology of *jaser* itself is subject to considerable doubt.

From the standpoint of weaselism, the striking claim was made recently in connection with the new production of *Porgy and Bess* that this is "the greatest American musical, by George Gershwin, the greatest American composer." Had the publicity read "one of the greatest," for both piece and composer, there would have been no issue. My own taste in Gershwin music runs to a musical he produced in collaboration, *The Song of the Flame,* which is seldom mentioned, or even listed, and never produced these days. It came out at the time of World War II, when the Soviets were viewed as our trusted allies, and it was natural that it would be soft-pedaled in the subsequent Cold War period; but even the "spirit of détente" has failed to bring it back.

At any rate, "greatest of American musicals" and "greatest of American composers" could run into serious competition with Victor Herbert's *Naughty Marietta* (Herbert was Irish-born, but his productive life was spent in the United States); Jerome Kern's *Show Boat;* Rodgers and Hammerstein's *South Pacific;* Lerner and Lowe's *My Fair Lady;* Leonard Bernstein's *West Side Story.* At the time of its first appearance, *Porgy and Bess* was described by its creator as "folk opera," by others as everything from "hybrid pseudo-opera" to "a Broadway musical with pretensions." Today, it is called "a thrilling, unforgettable event in American Opera or Broadway . . . Its soaring music remains some of the finest created for the American stage or opera."

Nolo contendere, as they say in the law courts; but viewpoints do change with the passing of time. Harold Schonberg, *The New York Times* music critic, is harsher than I in his judgment ("A Minority Report on Porgy," October 17, 1976): "commercial, slick, and sentimental," "basically false," "libretto and music fake"; Gershwin's talent is described as "clever, brittle, superficial." The "opera," in his opinion, is "commercial Broadway stuff, as the current revival only too mercilessly demonstrates." Needless to say, this review precipitated a long and bitter controversy, to which *The New York Times* devoted entire pages.

An interesting practice is reported from Hungary in connection with all forms of art, including works of literature. In that Communist country the arts and literature are heavily subsidized by the state, working through the Ministry of Culture. To pay for the subsidies, the Magyars have hit upon the expedient of imposing a so-called trash tax on all books, works of art, and musical recordings designated as artistically inferior by a board of experts. The tax is being currently imposed upon the novels of Agatha Christie, the music of Louis Armstrong, and the plays of Neil Simon, all of which are highly popular and therefore a bottomless reservoir of trash-tax forints.

Jane Trahey, who reports on this situation for *The New York Times,* wonders what the reaction of some of the producers of our literary, musical, and artistic best-sellers would be if they were to discover that a tax imposed upon their works went to make up the deficits of the Metropolitan Opera House, the New York Public Library, the Museum of Modern Art, the New York Philharmonic, and public TV (Richard Bach of *Jonathan Livingston Seagull,* Jacqueline Susann, and Xaviera Hollander, are selected as imaginary examples). Would they be happy at this index of popularity among the masses, or incensed at the label of artistic inferiority? At any rate, it's an ingenious idea, and one that might be considered by our own IRS. Out-and-out pornography, by the way, is completely excluded from presentation in Hungary, regardless of the revenue it would produce for worthy causes.

12 The Tongue of Sports

Is there any justification for entering this wide division of the English vocabulary under the heading of the performing arts? Perhaps so. Jack O'Brian, with his customary fervid imagination, labels the sports as the "Perspiration Arts." He also supplies an example of weasely use, not unconnected with the fact that he makes no secret of his strong likes and dislikes. Among the latter is sportscaster Howard Cossell, for whom he coins two unflattering designations: "Howie the Hoarse" and "The Mouth That Roared."

My own complaint is in connection with what has become a widespread practice on TV, that of abbreviating or omitting regularly scheduled programs in order to regale the viewers with a preceding game (be it baseball, football, hockey, golf, or basketball) right down to its bitter end. There is, however, no omission or cutting of commercials.

The genesis of this practice, which bids fair to place our rigidly allotted TV time schedule on a par with the sketchy practices of many foreign lands, is well known. Some years ago, there was a big football game in progress (I have forgotten the names of the teams, and it matters little to me whether my memory is refreshed or not). Only one or two minutes of playing time remained when the game was cut off from the viewers by the exact time schedule for the presentation of *Heidi,* an ideal picture for the kiddies, their fond mamas, and the PTA. As luck would have it, within that minute or two cut from the end of the game, one of the teams scored, reversing the previously foreseeable outcome. The protesting clamor from sports fans who had been intently watching the game was something fearsome. For days on end, the offending station was berated and abused. What did they mean by cutting off the crucial final minutes of that world-shaking game? Did they want to lose all their viewers and sponsors? It mattered little that children-oriented audiences and organizations defended *Heidi* and upheld the observance of the rigid time schedule. The sports fans (apparently there are more of them than there are mothers and teachers) won the argument. Since that time, games have been continued on the TV screen even when and if they overstep their allotted time, which they usually do.

The result is distressing to viewers who trust the printed announcement of programs and schedules, and tune in on "Sixty Minutes" only to find Georgia Tech and Kansas State still battling it out with five minutes to go that may easily stretch out into half an hour by reason of time-outs, and have to miss most or all of what they had been looking forward to. For good measure, the networks are not satisfied with merely bringing the game to its termination. They have to hold lengthy postmortems, with plenty of slow-motion replays and appropriate comments from "experts," to the distress of nonfans who are impatiently waiting for their curtailed program to begin. Because of the protests, the networks have recently sought a remedy. They announce that the program following the sports event will be presented in full as soon as the game is over, and keep their promise. But the remedy is perhaps worse than the disease, because they then have to reschedule all their later programs accordingly, thus affecting an even larger number of viewers, who, hours after the game, tune in on the eleven o'clock news and find *Love Story* still in progress.

My own suggested remedy, voiced to one of the offending networks and rejected by them, is to add half an hour to the normally scheduled time for their baseball, football, and other sports programs, and officially reschedule their other programs accordingly, and in time. If the game ends before the scheduled time does, it can easily be filled in, and commercial rights for it can easily be sold.

One additional complaint is in connection with baseball teams that are supposed to represent cities, but whose players are bought, sold, and transferred from every area in the country. I have often wondered how a New York viewer can take any personal pride out of Mets and Yankees who hail from all over creation. Since other countries have to ape all our bad habits, this system now prevails even for European, Asian, and South American soccer teams. How can an Italian soccer enthusiast enthuse over an "Italian" team that includes two Poles, three Germans, and one Frenchman?

A passing word may be added concerning the sudden American interest in soccer, a game previously scorned, to the point that when the women's soccer teams of France and Italy played an exhibition game on one of New York's East River islands, the stations did not bother to televise it or even take a few shots for their newscasts, despite the interest that would presumably have attached to the game by reason of its gentler-sex participants. The sudden reversal may have been due to the coming of Pelé, the recognized world star from Brazil. Soccer is now an admitted rival of the great traditional American games—football, baseball, and basketball. This marks another forward step in international communications and relations. An added bonus is that Pelé, in his commercials for American Express, insists on speaking his native Brazilian Portuguese, in the course of which he labels English "a foreign language."

The new popularity of soccer has not yet given rise to penetration of soccer terms into the general *colloquial*. First honors in this field still go to that old-time favorite, baseball. Consider, for example, this brief cross section of terms, culled from an excellent article on the subject by John O. Herbold II, which appeared in the May 1977 issue of *Verbatim*, a linguistic quarterly: "to have one (or two) strikes against one"; "to get to first base with someone"; "to be way off base" (or "way out in left field"); "to touch all bases"; "to get one's signals crossed"; "to throw someone a curve"; "to go to bat (or "to pinch hit") for someone"; "right off the bat"; "to call them as you see them"; "to hit them where they ain't"; "to have a lot on the ball."

Passing on to linguistic creativity, the terminology of sports is so abundant and varied that it has given rise to articles, books, lectures, and profound studies. That some of the terms should show weasely aspects and uses, along with creative features, is to be expected. "Slimnastics," for example, has recently been advanced for a new type of gymnastics, with the implied promise that it will slim you down. There is "zennis," a touted new form of training for tennis larded with Zen meditation. A new use has been found for "passing" at a football game; it is not the old and well-known forward pass, but consists of picking up a girl (any girl) and passing her through the audience, from spectator to spectator, until the fans tire of the new sport or the victim collapses.

A brand-new sports dictionary, over five hundred pages in length, has recently been published by Merriam-Webster. In addition to listing older and better-known terms in various fields, it offers several new ones. Reviewing it for *The New York Times*, Theodore Bernstein presents a cross section (incidentally coining a word himself, when he speaks of the Webster's "Sportsdic"). "Screwgy" for the antiquated "screwball" is one sample; the confusing confusion of "fallaway slide," "fadeaway slide," and "hook slide" is another. There is the "designated hitter" of the American League, not recognized by the National League. There is the former "broad jump" that became a "long jump," and the children's "hop, skip, and jump" that turned into "hop, step, and jump," and finally into "triple jump." "Sudden death" varies in its acceptance according to the sport involved, and "academic assault" is not something that happens in the halls of ivy, but on the fencing floor. Appropriately, Bernstein concludes that the "Sportsdic" omits today's most important word in sports: "commercialism."

But Bernstein and "Sportsdic" are far from exhausting the topic. Other sources supply us with "redneck" (a hothead); "flannel-mouth" (a player who shoots his mouth off); "bench jockey" (a player who sits on the bench, but rides the opposing team); "redshirt" (or "redfoot"; a player who defers his eligibility for one year; the designation is due to the fact that when practicing, aspirant players wear red shirts); "grand slam" (normally a bridge term; a home run hit when bases are full).

Roger Harris supplies "weak side backliner blitz," which he does not define, and "he came to play," which he calls "sentimental nonsense." Hockey, he says, which is a very simple game (just get the little rubber object into the other guy's net), is complicated by terms like "red line," "blue line," "icing," and "forechecking," which any watcher is free to ignore. What he really objects to is football's "hang time," the time it takes between the punting of a ball and its coming down. Why, he wonders, don't the sports announcers say that the ball stayed in the air for six seconds instead of: "He had real good hang time on that one: six seconds"; or "That's what the coaches like to see —plenty of that old hang time"? He then goes on to hypothesize what would have been done with "hang time" had it then been available to Nixon and his crowd, who favored "game plan." John Ehrlichman, talking about Pat Gray, would not have used "twisting slowly in the wind," but "Let's make sure Pat gets plenty of hang time." And John Mitchell would have said: "I guess we could stonewall it provided the hang time wasn't too long."

One recent news item concerned itself with "autogenic training," a form of self-hypnosis, said to be in vogue in the USSR, along with conventional hypnosis, for the purpose of boosting athletic performance. This "psyching-up" method has been in use since the 1972 Olympics in Munich. Dr. William Kroger, whose *Clinical and Experimental Hypnosis* is the most up-to-date book on the subject, claims that the main characteristic of the process consists of inducing a Yogalike state in the athletes, building up conditioning reflexes that permit them to perform without fear, anxiety, or tension, allowing full play to the body's "supermaximum potentials." Interestingly, there is a report from England of a similar device, but of a tranquilizing kind, designed to allay the stage fright of actors and singers so that they will give their best possible performance.

Violence and hooliganism are rife in sports, both among players and among spectators, as they are in the real life of which they are a segment, or, for that matter, in movies and TV programs. During the Ali-Norton fight at Yankee Stadium, mobs of marauding youths molested and mugged spectators in full view of the police, who were busy demonstrating against the loss of some of their privileges. During the American League pennant contest, Yankee fans amused themselves hurling empty bottles at opposing Kansas City players, then celebrated the Yankees' victory by ripping up sections of the turf and tearing apart the metal screen behind home plate. At a football game between the New York Jets and the New England Patriots at Foxboro Stadium near Boston, one fan fell out of the top stands, two suffered fatal heart attacks, and forty-nine were arrested for drunkenly attacking friends and strangers; a crippled fan's wheelchair was stolen, and thirty persons required hospital treatment. Things are just as bad in Europe, where they have to have protective moats to insulate players from irate fans.

Pleas for rationality and decorum have been to no avail.

Commercialism in sports is at its apex when it comes to betting. Here we find, as betting terminology is reported upon in a *New York Times* feature article, a wealth of understatement that seems designed to ensnare the innocent first-time bettor, and is to that extent weasely in the highest degree, however much it may be sanctified by racetrack usage. Consider, for example, that "small nickel" refers to a $500 bet, "big nickel" to a $5,000 bet. "Buck" is a wager of $100, but a wager of $1,000 can be either a "big one" or a "dime." One wonders to what extent novices may be taken in by this sort of thing; but then, what business do novices have in this field?

"Action" is the term for betting, but movies and TV have familiarized us with that one ("where the action is at"). "Beard," which in Hollywood parlance is a friend acting as a front for a married man who is carrying on an extramarital romance, is used in somewhat similar fashion in betting circles: he is the agent who "moves the action," or lays a wager, for another person who wants to conceal his identity. A "dog" is an underdog team. An "edge" is a betting advantage, real or imaginary, gained on information not generally known. "Vigorish" is the bookie's commission percentage (but it has been known to penetrate other underworld circles and indicates the percentage of a business's profits that racketeers charge for "protection"). A "runner," as might be expected, is a courier who works for a bookie, accepts wagers, pays off winners, and collects from losers. The sports bettors are known as the "Players" (capitalized so as not to be confused with players in the field). The "point spread" is the difference between points added to an underdog or subtracted from a football or basketball favorite to equalize the contest for betting purposes. But there can be added stipulations, when bets on a game are subject to special conditions, as whether a certain (on-the-field) player competes.

One final, international consideration: despite the fact that sporting terminology is perhaps the most idiomatic division of language, the ease with which sports terms pass from one language to another probably outstrips that of any other vocabu-

r, save perhaps the scientific. Our baseball ter-
has infiltrated the tongues of countries where the
become truly popular (particularly Japanese and
o an unbelievable degree.

But we, too, import from others. Bernstein, for instance, reports *piste* (the French term for "track") as having found its way
into English, following at a distance of centuries such French
loan-words as the "love" of tennis (*l'oeuf,* "the egg," or zero)
and "tennis" itself (*tenez,* "take this," "here you are," as you
serve).

On the other hand, as I listened to a recording of a popular
French song, I was mystified by one word I had never heard
before. It sounded like gro-GHEE. When I finally called for help
on a native Frenchman who also happened to be a sports fan-
cier, he smiled as he explained, "That's your own English
'groggy,' applied to a prizefighter who is about to suffer *le
knockout.*"

13 Press and Magazines— Modus Operandi

Books are as old as human civilization. But the modern book industry is something Gutenberg would hardly have dreamed of when he started it on its career. Books often serve as a medium for weasel words and practices, but in a more subdued fashion than the press, particularly of the daily variety, which, in its own way, flaunts weaselism to the same extent as the radio-TV complex.

There is one feature of presentation, almost universal in daily newspapers, far too frequent in magazines and reviews, that lends itself to criticism. Why do our major dailies find it necessary, or even expedient, to crowd into their front pages too many items that have to be continued on inner pages, often to the reader's great discomfort? From page 1, the item you are reading is continued on page 23 or 54, which may even be in another section of the paper. The break is not usually made at the end of a paragraph, but often comes in the middle of a sentence, even of a word. This is both messy and irritating. Its only excuse seems to be that the editors wish to give front-page prominence to as many items as possible, so as to catch the reader's eye and hold his breathless interest. What they succeed in doing is annoying the reader. Is it their desire to intersperse the reading matter with advertisements so that one may not be tempted to lay the entire advertising section aside, as happens with the help-wanted and real-estate sections if one is not looking for a job or a house? The same goal might be achieved by treating the first ten or twelve pages as front pages, each carrying an item of interest in its entirety, each flanked by appropriate ads. One is nostalgically reminded of some old-style British newspapers, where the front page was devoted exclusively to ads, often of the personal-message variety, and you had to go on to the inner pages to find the news, in orderly and complete arrangement.

Magazines generally follow a similar practice, shorn of the front-page feature, starting an article on one page and directing you to another page, much farther along, for its continuation. Here the interspersing of reading material and advertising seems to be the primary goal. A correspondent says to columnist Helen Botte, "I spend more time searching for the complete article than I do reading it," and goes on to complain that a major story, usually buried in the middle of the magazine where you must search for it after having read the cover blurb, is continued on page 106, then on page 165; stashed between those pages are the "advertising supplements," numbered like P.S. 1–22, which are intermingled with pages having no numbers at all. Helen Bottel sedately replies that if a more logical procedure were followed it would upset advertisers.

There are notable and praiseworthy exceptions to this system. *Reader's Digest* and *U.S. News & World Report* come to mind; there articles are continued on immediately following pages until they are completed. They, too, carry advertising; but, as brought out by the editor of *U.S.N. & W.R.* in one of the most pointed TV commercials to come to my notice, they aim "to spare their readers useless news, and their advertisers useless readers."

A charge of "sexism" against some popular magazines is voiced by another reader. The magazines, she claims, put a false emphasis on the idea of physical beauty by stressing the need for constant beauty care. If a person were to follow all the "commandments for total grooming," she could neither work at a full-time job nor take care of a home and children. The magazines, she charges, imply that a woman's sole worth is to be sexually attractive to men.

An implied criticism of our magazines comes from a foreign source. *Sputnik*, a monthly digest of the Soviet press and literature, which is available in English, French, and German as well as Russian-language editions, claims it "gives a refreshing break from infantile glamorization of sex and violence. 'Culture' is not a dirty word, and when a *Sputnik* article is 'corny,' it's really about corn."

The methods by which magazines and newspapers obtain their news and photos come in for strong criticism from the objects of the activities of news reporters and cameramen, even when they are not of the *paparazzi* or ultra pushy variety. After a mine accident in Tower City, Pennsylvania, a few years ago about a hundred such camped around the scene of the tragedy and turned it into a circus, asking bereaved relatives of the victims how they felt, and rushing after the bodies of the dead and the sorrowing kinfolk "like vultures moving in for the kill," in the words of an eyewitness.

Another criticism of news treatment (this applies mainly to dailies) is the way the news item is written up, with a paragraph that is meant to be startling and give you a nutshell view, later expanded, with details that are often repetitious. For this, instead of a logical unfolding, the responsibility seems to lie with the schools of journalism: "Make your point at the very outset! Be sensational! Capture and imprison the reader!" seems to be the underlying philosophy. Impressionism takes the upper hand over logical development.

An even more serious criticism is connected with the endless repetition of information with which the reader is usually already familiar, as contrasted with new and relevant information the reader really wants. At the time of the Arab oil embargo, there was considerable loose talk about the United States sending armed forces into one or more of the Arab countries to seize the oil wells by force of arms, in much the same way that the British and French had tried to wrest the Suez Canal away from Egypt's Nasser when he "nationalized" that vital waterway. For this procedure, there had been some moral and legal justification in the fact that the treaty signed by Egypt, Britain, and France at the time of the building of the canal definitely gave the two European governments the right to operate the canal for a specified number of years before Egypt took over, and that time was still some ten years in the offing. The question arose in some minds, including mine: "What are the arrangements entered into by the American-European oil interests, which first discovered the oil and put the wells into profitable operation, and the individual Arab countries on whose soil the wells are located? Do they call for ownership and operation in perpetuity; or for a limited number of years; or is ownership vested in the local countries and governments, with definite rights of expropriation?" Doubtless a question with many angles, and quite possibly with different answers from country to country, particularly in view of the political changes that had occurred in many of the Arab nations. Still, it seemed to be the right of American citizens, for whom so many rights to know are claimed, to be informed, even in a general way, about the moral and legal aspects of the matter before any hostilities might be initiated. No organ of the press, to my knowledge, presented anything on the subject. One great New York daily, to which I suggested that an article by an expert in the field (certainly not I) might be in order, left my inquiry unanswered. Yet many news items of far lesser national interest or significance are described and commented upon *ad nauseam.*

At the time of the 1976 primaries, many press organs, both dailies and magazines, ran the results as soon as they became known, even if incomplete. Some ran periodical tabulations of delegate counts. What the tabulations did not include was the popular vote for each state primary, something the reader could have done for himself if he had thought of it in time. One magazine to which I subscribe, noted for its accurate statistical tabulations in all kinds of fields, was requested to add to its delegate tabulation that of total popular vote. This would have led to a true understanding of the real standing of the candidates within their own parties, and even later, when the designated candidates would be squared off against each other. The request was turned down, on the ground that some states did not give out their popular-vote figures (actually, I believe Texas was the only state where this happened). Was this a slight infringement of "the people's right to know" all the news that may be really meaningful for an intelligent analysis of what goes on?

But the most important weasely feature connected with the press media appears, in my mind, under the constitutional guarantee of "freedom of the press." Broadly, this means that anyone who has the means can own and run a newspaper or magazine, and advance and advocate his or her own views, even if these oppose the established order, provided the person does not sponsor actual violence or voice the grossest forms of vituperation or obscenity. Within these limitations, one is free to attack institutions, groups, and individuals, so long as he or she steers clear of actual libel or slander, in which case one is open to civil action for damages.

This leaves the press free to conduct private investigations into the behavior of institutions, groups, and individuals, and bring its findings to the public at large. But there are two essential differences between investigation by government agencies, such as the office of the attorney general, the district attorney, and, on occasion and indirectly, a congressional body, and investigation by the press. The former leads to indictment, prosecution, and jury trial under rigid rules of evidence. The second leads to public exposure, which may in turn, but not necessarily, be picked up by a government agency and lead to the same things. If it does not, the rigid rules of evidence do not apply. The victim of a press investigation that is biased or baseless ordinarily has no recourse save the civil libel suit for damages. The witnesses not only do not appear; they may also remain unidentified. The inquiring reporter, according to this interpretation of "freedom of the press," can destroy a person's reputation, happiness, even life, on the basis of what a court of law would throw out as "hearsay" evidence. The reporter may not be questioned as to his sources or methods of acquiring the information he divulges. The district attorney, police detective, or FBI man may be, and is so questioned. His witnesses must be identified and produced, which is why so many criminal cases go by default because the witnesses are afraid to appear.

There are important angles of "freedom of the press" that are connected with problems of national security, as well as ethical and legal standards. A widespread weekly supplement *(Parade)* answers an inquiry from a curious reader, who knew (how did she know?) that Marlon Brando had checked into a hospital, but was told he was not registered there when she phoned in. "Does he use his real name or a fake one when he is checked into a hospital?" Reply: "Brando used the name Jim Ferguson when checking into the hospital." Is this the type of information that should be divulged? A hospital patient, no matter how popular, should have the right to get away from his fans for the duration of his stay.

One of the most famous of our columnists, who perennially boasts of having access to all kinds of official and unofficial sources (how?), but at the same time thunders out against FBI and CIA abuses of constitutional rights of citizens (such as the Ellsberg break-in), seemingly got a secretary in his pay to rifle the files of a senator he wanted to "get" (and "got"). Worse yet, he gave a jocular account of a harmless conversation between

Brezhnev and Kosygin that had been obtained by bugging the limousine in which they were riding to their masseuse. This had been reported by a CIA operative to his superiors in Washington. The leaking of this seemingly innocent colloquial interchange probably led to the exposure and arrest, possibly death, of the operative, since the number of people having access to that official limousine was very limited. This, of course, is only a surmise.

There is more than a surmise, however, that Daniel Schorr's revelation and subsequent publication of names and locations of CIA operatives in foreign countries, "somehow" leaked to Schorr from the files of a secret congressional committee investigating the CIA, was responsible for the ambushing and killing, very soon thereafter, of two of the operatives whose identity and location had been divulged. Yet a congressional committee investigating the matter, to which Schorr refused to reveal the source of his leak, found no grounds to hold him in contempt. One is tempted to compare this leniency with the case of G. Gordon Liddy, who was sentenced to an indeterminate jail sentence of up to thirty years for refusing to reveal what he knew about the Watergate break-in to Judge John Sirica, who held him in contempt.

There are other angles to the doctrine of "freedom of the press." Once upon a time, this meant that newspapers refused to publish letters from their readers, however informative and reasonably couched, that conflicted with their editorial policies. As exchange professor in Portugal in 1961, I was amazed to read an editorial condemnation of Portuguese "racism" in *The New York Times.* My own Portuguese experience included visits to schools and universities where black Portuguese students from Angola and Mozambique lived side by side with their white Portuguese counterparts on terms of absolute equality and friendship; a luncheon with the Portuguese minister of education, who was an East Indian from Goa (speaking, incidentally, the most beautiful Portuguese I have ever heard); even a black priest officiating at the all-white Lisbon church I attended. My letter attesting to these facts was turned down. Fortunately, it was later published by *The New York Herald-Tribune.* On another occasion, *The New York Times Magazine* published an article by my Columbia colleague Henry Steele Commager, singing the praises of the federal government as the protector of the individual's rights as opposed to state governments. Again I sent in a letter, which was turned down. This time I exercised my own "freedom of the press," and included my rejected letter in my book *The America We Lost,* with a heading to the effect that the *Times,* as a privately owned newspaper, was completely within its rights in rejecting a letter not in conformity with its editorial policy.

It would be presumptuous on my part to claim that this episode had anything to do with the change that swept over the media shortly thereafter. Today, major press media accept and publish letters, even paid articles, that run counter to their editorial policies. TV goes them one better, inviting and presenting opposing viewpoints to their nightly editorials. "Freedom of the press" has become far freer than it used to be, at least in this important respect.

There are, however, other weasely aspects that are still current. Many press organs display attitudes that can only be described as hopelessly partial in connection with international affairs, and particularly foreign governments of the dictatorial variety. Take, for example, this headline from a column by Joseph Kraft: LESSER MEN WILL EXPLOIT MAO'S GREAT FREE SPIRIT. Great perhaps in the same sense that Genghis Khan, Tamerlane, and other conquerors of the past, down to Napoleon and Hitler, were great. Free? Think of the great purge of Chinese thought, of the Cultural Revolution, and the millions who lost their lives. Something similar occurs with some of the Soviet leaders, Castro of Cuba, Torrijos of Panama, Tito of Yugoslavia, even Kim Il Sung of North Korea, whose praises are often sung in full-page paid ads in the Sunday *Times.* Compare this with the treatment generally accorded to the late Chiang Kai-shek, the late Franco of Spain, Park of South Korea, Smith of Rhodesia, the Greek colonels, the present government of Chile, all reprehensible in some respects, but no more so than their leftist counterparts. Shall we say that the press follows official directives, from Washington or elsewhere? Mass murderers are tolerated and even praised when it suits someone's purpose, deplored and condemned when it does not.

The 1976 election campaign called for all sorts of investigations, including Ford's golfing vacations when he accepted the hospitality of a friend of long standing. The New York City situation was deplored, and a Republican administration blamed for not pouring billions in federal funds into the city to rescue it from its own follies, which go all the way back to when former Mayor Abraham Beame was comptroller and John Lindsay and Robert Wagner were mayors. But no one calls for a thorough investigation of those administrations.

At the time when Ford turned down an appeal for billions to rescue New York, one press organ came out with a blaring headline: FORD TO NEW YORK: DROP DEAD! Ford had never said anything of the sort. Yet that headline cropped up again and again in the course of the 1976 presidential campaign. Even Albert Shanker, the respected head of the teachers' union, in his advertisement column of October 3, 1976, in the Sunday *Times,* brought it up in this weasely form: "He [the President] has to stop telling them [the cities], as one headline put it, to 'drop dead.' "

14 Press and Magazines— Creativity (for Better or for Worse)

In this more cheerful area, we discover abundant and imaginative coinages of new words and expressions, along with grammatical irregularities of a deliberate kind. Some of them are barbed.

Most prolific in this field is columnist Jack O'Brian, who has fallen heir to the mantle of Walter Winchell. Consider his use of "to daddy," for the more common but less graceful "to father" (Franco Nero, he announces, "daddied" a baby with Vanessa Redgrave), and "to pulitzer" (" 'South Pacific' pulitzered in 1950"); his "unchic surgery" for a hernia operation; "preggy" for pregnant; "freedom of depression" for pornography; "atomic balm" for Count Basie's music; and "prism pallor" for Andy Warhol in civilian clothes. He calls the *National Lampoon Calendar* for 1976 a "soul screamer book-of-the-month." "Artsy-tartsy" is his description of Jacqueline Kennedy Onassis's editorial writing.

He is not fond of Barbra Streisand, whom he labels "La Strident"; or of Howard Cosell, whom he calls a "cliché-ridden nonsequiturarian." Tom Jones he describes as "hip-swishing." Slim and slender Jane Fonda, he says, has weight problems by reason of compulsive "noshing" (this he did not coin himself; it is a borrowing from Yiddish, like his "meshpuchah" for engagement gift, which I have been unable to trace in our most recent dictionaries, even of slang).

For a fashion show he coins "avant duds." He describes at length Henny Youngman's gripes with Ma Bell, which paid Henny only $2,500 for initiating its dial-a-joke series, and with Rin-Tin-Tin producers, who are suing him for plagiarism (in a title?) in connection with his spoof title *Won-Ton-Ton.* He also informs us that the nonalcoholic version of the "Bloody Mary," after a sacrilegious interlude as "Virgin Mary," has finally settled down in some localities into an acceptable "Bloody Shame."

Other columnists give proof of creative mentalities, though not to the same extent. Joseph Kraft coins "Presigressional Leadership" for the sort of thing the President and Congress should produce in concert. The late Peter Lisagor called the Washington reporters (this presumably included himself) "The Hounds of Disasterville." Ann Landers has "people bags," instead of doggie bags, into which restaurant leftovers are piled for human rather than canine consumption. Marvin Kitman gives us "underwhelming," along with an expletive of real disgust: "Yechhh!" *Dark Victory* is described by Robert Rose as a "real four-handkerchief special." Louis Feuer coins and defines "telegogue": one who selects and edits news and emits "two-minute capsules of what they call analysis." Some of the quips seem largely unconscious, as when Xaviera Hollander speaks of "the Best Part of a Man." Others are quite deliberate, as when *Graffiti* reminds us that when we resist temptation, it may never come again.

Under the heading of "Adverteasement" there is a UPI account of a hoax designed by the *Salina* (Kansas) *Journal* to ascertain whether anybody really reads the ads. It offered for sale "a green gitzensnorker with power flaker, and two matching frammelists including automatic bleem." But a reply quickly came from an alert reader, who, describing himself as a "purchasing swapskeller," offered in trade a "fanning mill

fingpong manipulator with shakeling strawmoling parts missing," inquiring at the same time whether the "bleem" has a
"long-stoke gismokitchet."

We have, finally, an etymology of sorts for the puzzling *papa-
razzo* (intrusive, offensive press photographer), for which neither Italian *papera* ("duck"; also slangy for "blooper") nor
French-English *papier-paper* seems to supply the clue. According to one source, it was invented by Federico Fellini, who
immortalized it in his 1970 *La Dolce Vita*, and was first applied
by him to one of the hustling photographers on Via Veneto who
seek pictures of stars and other celebrities. But the question still
remains: "Why did he call him by that name?"

As against deliberate or accidental usages that might lend
themselves to the charge of weaselism, does the press commit
bloopers in spelling, grammar, or logic that betoken ignorance
or carelessness?

One of my local papers carries an article on what they meant
to be "Angola's Tragic Troika," the three factions that fought it
out to a standstill after the Portuguese left that country. The
body of the article contains seven correct spellings of "Angola"
as against a single "Agnola," but the headline reads: ANGELO'S
TRAGIC TROIKA. Another local daily states that "police dis-
bursed the students" (what they meant was "dispersed"). Our
leading local daily states that "Gunmen miss ex-Turkish Premier [this was Ecevit] at Rally." Did Ecevit cease to be a Turk,
or merely cease to be premier? In an editorial we find: "Singling
out Actibank as the chief villain . . . is itself incredulous." Yet
we deplore the fact that high-school students confuse such
words as "incredulous" and "incredible." Elsewhere: "The horrors a modern sniper can penetrate [perpetrate?] upon society"
and "The character is extremely well profited [profiled?] by a
group of psychiatrists." In another editorial we read "conjec-
tive" for "conjectural." Still elsewhere, a letter is allowed to
appear over the signature of a writer who is described (or de-

scribes himself; we can't tell which) as a representative of the "B'nai B'rith Anti-Definitive League." And in another editorial about Evel Knievel: "He's alive and considerably *more richer* than before he *catapaulted* into the air over the gorge." In a later editorial in the same daily, Billy Carter is said not to have the political charisma that *catapaulted* his elder brother from relative obscurity into the presidency, indicating that the error is not due to a misprint. The following, however, may well be one: "If more people in Germany had written letters to the editors opposing Hitler's rise to power, *we* would never have reached the top, and the course of the world would have been changed." Strangely, the item may be correct even as it stands.

A curious distortion of logic, sanctified by use in a once popular song ("And them spurs ain't so very far from wrong!") is repeated by the *Newark Star-Ledger*'s highly cultured educational editor, Robert J. Braun: "Although the motives might be questioned, the argument is probably not far from wrong." Both in the song and in Braun's piece, the meaning is, of course, "not far from right."

Are these examples too localized? Jack Anderson accuses President Carter of spending much of his time "pouring" over stacks of memoranda, and adds that such duties should be "relegated" (delegated?) to a secretary. David Broder says that "Some of these men *emphasized* [empathized?] with the anguish the President felt." One of Jack O'Brian's columns says that "what people do or say on a given day *bares* scant resemblance to what they see of themselves on the evening news." In an editorial reproduced from *The Christian Science Monitor* (September 25, 1975) there appears: "For a long time the gradual post-Victorian lifting of taboos in literature and the other arts was justified in terms of honestly depicting human experience rather than *blinkeredly* falsifying it." Peter Lisagor wrote in one of his columns: "citizens with whom he *shaked* hands or *greeted.*" O'Brian reports from Westbury Music Fair: "Sammy Davis billed as the *most complete* entertainer of his time." And both Joseph Kraft and Jack Anderson, in their respective columns for the same day, make a strange use of "savvy" as an adjective. The former says, "Savvy Americans know that . . ."; the latter, "Schlesinger, the savvy former Defense Secretary . . ."

We can urge our students to watch less TV and read more. But read what?

The items above may have created the impression that our daily press is a cultural wasteland. Such an impression would be erroneous. There is an abundance of good, careful, literate, even literary writers among the news staffs and columnists. In fact, some are constantly criticized and satirized for being too cultured. Consider this quip by Bill Vaughan: "After you have gained confidence by doing the cross-word puzzle in ink, you can move on to reading William Buckley without a dictionary."

Buckley is more than a careful writer. He is a fastidious writer, given to using exactly the right word in the right place, even if the right word happens to be unknown to 99 percent of his readers. There is no question that the compilers and publishers of comprehensive dictionaries owe much to Buckley in the way of expanded sales. So, for that matter, do his readers, in the way of expanded vocabularies. In one of his columns, in which he discussed the case of Robert Redford versus the CIA, I ran into two words I had not seen before in English, "anfractuous" and "energumen." But their cognates, *anfrattuoso* and *energumeno,* are more widely used in my native Italian, so I did not have to look them up in Webster's *Third International.*

Buckley's fellow-columnist and fellow-conservative, James J. Kilpatrick, once devoted his entire column to "Watching Buckley's Language." Beginning with "opsimathy," a quality Buckley had attributed to Rockefeller, Kilpatrick says he consulted everyone in the editorial room of *The Washington Star,* then went on to confer with Martin Agronsky, Hugh Sidey, Peter Lisagor, and Carl Rowan, journalists of vast erudition. No one knew what it meant (the ability to learn late in life). From an anthology of Buckley's writings, Kilpatrick culls such words as "osmotic," "ecdysiasm," "hubristic," "animadversion," "oetiose," "lubricious," "androgynous," "velleity," and many more of the same ilk, along with phrases such as "to immanentize the eschaton," which he (Kilpatrick, not Buckley) translates as "to cause to inhere in the worldly experience and subject [verb; stress on the last syllable] to human dominion that which is beyond time, and therefore extraworldly." Kilpatrick expresses some alarm at the fact that the Buckleyesque vocabulary shows signs of being contagious, citing the "celebrification" of the *Columbia Journalism Review*, and, worse yet, a piece on Patty Hearst composed by George Will (a columnist and conservative in his own right) to the effect that "Patty's arrest provided a coda to a decade of political infantilism, the exegesis of which could be comprehended as a manifestation of bourgeois *Weltanschauung*," and prophesies that the junior pundit will go a long way. He concludes that "without the assiduous peregrinations of the discoverers of 'opsimathy,' through the labyrinthine mazes of lexicography, we might dwell forever in the simplistic pages of Dick and Jane and Spot, their ubiquitous canine." And what a horrible fate that would be!

Other literate writers can sometimes get themselves entangled in the underbrush of their own syntax. Consider this description, appearing in *The New York Times Book Review* (November 13, 1977): "a young woman in love with an artist who in turn is loved by a rear admiral twice her age." Once upon a time it would have been fairly safe to assume that both the artist and the rear admiral were males. But these days there are plenty of woman artists, and even woman rear admirals. Also, lesbianism and homosexuality have come out of the closet. Therefore, does the "who" of the subordinate clause refer to the young woman or to the artist? Even a comma between "artist" and "who" would have helped!

15 The Wonderful World of Books

The other branch of the print media consists of books, which display some features in common with daily newspapers, weeklies, and magazines, but also some essential differences, that have a definite bearing on the nature and extent of weasely content.

The daily, weekly, even monthly or quarterly, is meant to be primarily a disseminator of news, the more current the better. The book, which far antedates the newspaper or magazine, only occasionally concerns itself with news of current import, though it can often be historically slanted on the modern side. It normally restricts itself to one topic. It is not dependent on advertising to cover part or most of its running expenditures, but upon its readership. If there are publicitarian excesses connected with it, they usually appear outside of the book itself.

The book industry is as much a business, in its own way, as is the production and sale of steel, automobiles, or oil. It must be run as such in order to prosper. This means that the book publisher has to be concerned with profits and losses. The field is highly competitive. Authors in all sorts of lines of endeavor often wonder why their offerings are turned down. The answer is generally one, and only one. The publisher doesn't think the book will sell sufficiently to cover expenses and bring in a profit.

One may argue with his judgment, but not with his motive.

There are, of course, cases where the publisher thinks the book is good, but not suited for his own special outlets and the readers he caters to. Conversely, a publisher's editor may feel compelled to accept a book against which his literary critical judgment revolts. One editor whom I was visiting in his office pointed to a book on his desk, printed and ready for distribution. It was about flying saucers. "I feel as though I wouldn't want to touch it with a ten-foot pole," he confessed. "But make no mistake about it. It will sell!" It did.

Entire books could be written about publishers' errors of judgment, but they are the first to admit that they may be in error. A rejection is not the end of the world, and plenty of books (even some of mine) have gone on to success after several rejections.

The matter of a book's timeliness often crops up to upset the best-laid plans of authors and publishers. Ultratimely books can be "written" (if this is the appropriate word) quite fast these days, with the help of tape recordings, skilled secretaries, and ghostwriters. They can also be printed and bound fast, at added expense to the publisher. But this happens only to books for which vast sales are expected. Normally, a period of six to twelve months has to elapse between the signing of a contract and the delivering of a complete manuscript, and another six to twelve months before the printed book is out. In one or two years' time, a topic that is very timely can lose all or most of its public appeal. A publisher whose means are limited contracted for and brought out an excellent book on the Biafran War in Nigeria nearly two years after the war had ended. By that time, people had forgotten what and where Biafra, and even Nigeria, were.

As of August 1976, it was announced that the *Scribner-Bantam English Dictionary* going to press in September of that year would have to base itself on Gallup and other polls, and designate James Carter as the thirty-ninth President of the

United States. Fortunately for them, the election results bore
them out. But this was not known until two months after the
announcement. It was suggested by the editor of one newspaper in which the item appeared that some confusion might
result if some far-in-the-future prober should find this reference
along with old copies of the *Literary Digest* and the *Chicago
Tribune*, indicating, respectively, that Landon was our thirty-
first and Dewey our thirty-fourth President.

A related problem is that far too many people of prominence
in various fields, especially politics and the arts, feel it is incumbent upon them to write books of memoirs, or to describe in
detail some episode with which they were connected (Watergate is a glaring example). Often they are pressed into doing this
by profit-hungry publishers who offer huge advances that the
authors can't resist. At other times, they are impelled by motives of self-justification. Books of this type, brought out by the
"fast" method described above, usually sell well because the
episode is still fresh in people's minds. Almost as often, they
clutter up the literary scene for a short time, then sink back into
semioblivion and remainder counters. They may be of value to
future historians, who will, however, have to sift out both facts
and motivation. They add little to our stock of true literature.
Some (by no means all) of their writers are only semiliterate and
semiarticulate. But if a profit is smelled, there is an army of
highly literate editors, copy editors, secretaries, ghostwriters,
translators, and other professionals ready to step into the
breach, and these are placed at the authors' disposal, regardless
of cost. After all, modern book publishing is run as a business,
and success in business attends only relentless efficiency.

Before we go on to describe what can be and often is weasely
about the way books are publicized and marketed, here are a
few picturesque expressions peculiar to the trade: a "vanity
publisher" is one who publishes a book for a subsidy that regularly more than covers the expenses (some subsidies, paid by

foundations and educational institutions that for reasons of scientific or institutional prestige want a book to be published that will definitely not sell enough copies to pay its way, are quite legitimate; this includes the activities of most university presses). The vanity publisher of whom other publishers speak with scorn is one who accepts and publishes, for a financial consideration, a book that he knows has little merit, but that the writer desperately wants to see appear in print with his name on it. A "penalty book" (I must confess that I had never heard the expression until this description was applied by its publisher to one of my own books, which, incidentally, did not do at all badly when it appeared) is one that the publisher accepts in order to get the author to sign a contract for another book that the publisher really wants.

There are a couple of expressions seemingly coined by book reviewers: "fi-fi" for finance fiction, a fictional work dealing with doings in the world of finance, as applied by a reviewer to Paul Erdman's *The Billion Dollar Sure Thing;* "fi-fi" is apparently based on the earlier "sci-fi" for science fiction. "Fanzine," incidentally, is the contraction for "fan magazine," further defined by the Book-Ends editor of *The New York Times Book Review* as a "mass-circulation magazine devoted to news, gossip, puffery, about the doings of Liz, Jackie, Cher, and other divinities." "Semidocumentary," "nonfiction novel," even "faction" (for factual fiction) have been applied to such works as Truman Capote's *In Cold Blood* and Alex Haley's *Roots.* "Bogusity" (the quality of being bogus), appearing in the *New York Times Book Review* of November 6, 1977, in connection with T. E. Lawrence and Hugh Trevor-Roper, seems to be a reviewer's creation. One of our favorite book words, "best-seller," has been appropriated by the Russians, and appears as a single word, in Cyrillic characters, in the Russian-language version of *Sputnik* for July 1977 *("Sovetskie Bestsellery 70-go Godov").*

"Book-or" has been applied to a ghostwriter, and "book-ee" to the man describing himself to the ghostwriter who whips his story into acceptable literary shape. "Alibiography" was heard on the "Dean Martin Show," as applied to an autobiography that was full of excuses for the biographee's questionable behavior.

Books are written on every conceivable topic, including those specifically treated in this book. Weasely features appearing in their contents are therefore to be found under their specific headings, such as "advertising," "theater," "arts," "sciences," "sex," "Women's Lib," "education," etc. Here I shall restrict myself to weasel words and expressions used in connection with the publicity methods employed to stimulate the promotion and sale of books, either by publishers in their commercial advertising, by authors in their catchy titles, or by reviewers and people of note in their published judgments.

Beginning with the last, there is an item concerning Jessica Mitford, a highly successful author in her own right (*The American Way of Death*, for instance), who often receives unsolicited copies of books by authors not yet fully successful, with a request for a "quotable quote." Miss Mitford sent a quote to the effect that she thought one such book was "totally absorbing." The author wrote back that in publishers' experience this expression has been found to be not so effective as certain others, like "tremendously exciting and important," or "highly significant and compelling drama." This led Miss Mitford to suggest in turn that perhaps publishers might draw up a list of desirable phrases for use on book jackets, ranging all the way from "blockbuster" to the ineffective "totally absorbing," with a code number for each to simplify the process. *The New York Times Book Review* editor in charge of Book Ends, in turn, offered to tabulate and rank by popularity such a list if publishers would send in their preferences, and himself started the ball rolling by suggesting "riveting," "hypnotic," "pageturner," "a good read," "a gorgeous book." ("Can't-put-it-downer" is supplied by another reviewer in connection with William Safire's *Full Dis-*

closure. I may add that I have been at both ends of this game, supplying for the books of others and receiving for my own books "quotable quotes." While the practice is thoroughly legitimate, I consider its value to be limited, as compared with quotes from published reviews, into which the personal element of friendship and association (or, for that matter, dislike or enmity) doesn't usually enter. It may be added that in connection with a more recently published book, *A Fine Old Conflict,* in which she describes some of her former pro-Communist activities in California, Miss Mitford offers a fine coinage: "I fear we were awesomely self-righteous (or should it be *leftuous?*)"

The title of a book is something for which author and publisher are jointly responsible (some of the catchiest titles of my books have been supplied by highly ingenious publishers' editors). There is no doubt that the search for an attractive title often leads to weaselism of one kind or another.

In highly questionable taste is a title like David Hapgood's *The Screwing of the Average Man,* meaning the consumer; it antedated Carter's *Playboy* article, incidentally. There is a picture book on sex for children (and parents, by courtesy) titled *Show Me!,* which the youngsters are too prone to do anyhow. There is what might be called a "best-seller by linguistic misunderstanding" (deliberately induced?), like *Your Erroneous Zones* ("erroneous" and "erogenous," you know); the book is merely one of self-help for what concerns all parts of the human body. There is a question, too, whether *Shogun* may not be too close to "shotgun" for the understanding of the average bookbuyer. (But this is unlikely now that the book has been joined by a widely advertised game by the same title).

There are title plagiarisms and semiplagiarisms (but keep in mind that a title cannot be copyrighted, and may be appropriated by anyone who wants to use it). In this class we find *Jaws* followed at a distance by *The Jaws Log* (but this is an account of how the original picture was made); *The Bermuda Triangle* followed by *The Bermuda Triangle Mystery; I'm O.K., You're O.K.* followed by *I'm O.K., You're a Pain in the Neck.*

There is what might be called the "swiped cliché" title: *Are All Italians Lousy Lovers?; Too Much Anger, Too Many Tears; All the Strange Hours.* There is the super-impressive title: *The Poseidon Adventure; The Prometheus Crisis; The Maximus Poems; Sister X and the Victims of Foul Play.* There is the cutesy title, sometimes based on a pun: *The War Between the Tates; Nice Guys Finish Last; How the Good Guys Finally Won.* Dr. Seuss's "Please try to remember the first of Octember . . . when impossible wishes come true," a cutesy coinage based on a musical piece with a nice tune but somewhat silly words, seems to fit into this category. One is at a loss how to classify Tolkien's *The Hobbit* and *The Silmarillion,* which have not yet made the dictionaries but combine the trappings of sci-fi and fairy tales. There is even the double-barreled title: a *BLAST!,* followed by a colon, followed by a small *blast!*

The popularity of certain words in book titles tends to cast light upon current popular interest. Among books of a certain type, *The Story of—* and *Invitation to—* work well and are fairly legitimate (I cheerfully plead guilty to having been inspired by *The Story of Philosophy* in the choice of some of my own titles; *The History of—* is more formal and definitive, while *Story* is indicative of an easier, more colloquial, more popular treatment; I miss the distinction between the two English words in some of the foreign translations of my books).

To judge from the constant recurrence of certain words in book titles, the three things that are deemed to be uppermost in the mind of the present-day American reader are money, power, and totality (the last regularly expressed by its adjective, "total"). Almost in the same class is the joy(s) of something or other. Whether this is indicative of current preoccupations or states of mind is for the reader to judge. Here is a recent partial record:

Money: Galbraith's *Money;* Sylvia Porter's *Money Book;* Hailey's *The Moneychangers;* also *Supermoney, Blood and Money.*

Power: Korda's *Power! How to Get It, How to Use It;* Castaneda's *Tales of Power;* Mintz and Cohen's *Power, Incorporated;* Rifkin and Howard's *Redneck Power: The Wit and Wisdom of Billy Carter;* Leo Rosten's *The Power of Positive Nonsense;* Phyllis Schafly's *The Power of the Positive Woman;* also *Power Shift; The Power Lovers.*

Total: *Total Fitness; The Total Woman; The Total Beast* (title of a film George Peppard expects to produce and direct); *Total Impact* (name of a film dealing with the renovation of a tenement). Note that in *The TM Book,* the "T" stands not for "total," though that would be quite appropriate, but for "transcendental."

Joy(s) of: *Sports, Yiddish, Wine,* various national cookings, *Sex* (along with *Gay Sex, Lesbian Sex, Oral Love*).

Lastly, there is a synthesis that is imperfect, but close enough: Chesler and Goodman's *Women, Money and Power.* Another is Morgan's *Total Joy.*

The above categories seem to have displaced a former favorite, "How to—," which lent itself to a multitude of purposes. All I have found in recent times is Jong's *How to Save Your Own Life;* Newman and Berkowitz's *How to Take Charge of Your Life;* and *How to Make Yourself Miserable.*

Love, a perennial favorite, still blooms: Wilde's *Love's Tender Fury;* Matthews's *Love's Avenging Heart* and *Love's Wildest Promise,* Ashton's *Love's Triumphant Heart;* Blake's *Love's Wild Desire.*

One category that is seldom mentioned by name, though it seems to preoccupy many minds, is that of forcible rape *(Against Our Will).* It has been suggested that the interest in this topic may in part be due to a subconscious fascination, or fascinated fear, engendered in the liberated woman of today by a hidden desire to be subdued by a conquering male; but in view of the often revolting aspects of the phenomenon, coupled with the distinct and ever-present possibility that the action may be followed by the murder of the victim, this theory seems highly exaggerated. The fascination is more likely to be exerted on some unstable masculine minds by lengthy newspaper accounts and by certain movie scenes.

A few other uses of words in titles, though not so widespread as the ones mentioned above, are "affirmative" (Glazer's *Affirmative vs. Basic Discrimination*); "save your life" used as an adjective compound *(The Save Your Life Diet);* "liberation" *(Animal Liberation;* note also *P.E.T.,* which does not deal with animals, but serves as an abbreviation for *Parent Effectiveness Training);* "body" (Wittig's *The Lesbian Body*); "tomorrow" as an adjective *(The Tomorrow File,* a view of a future society); "morality" *(The Morality of Consent);* even "60 seconds" (a real quickie: *Sixty Seconds to Mind Expansion,* described as a modification of TM). There is also *All Creatures* (or *All Things*), followed by *Great and Small, Bright and Beautiful, Wise and Wonderful;* but they are all by the same author, James Herriot, who was inspired by a hymn composed by Cecil Frances Alexander that has for its fourth line "The Lord God Made Them All."

Reviewers cannot be blamed for occasionally waxing satirical about the books they are forced to read and review. David Murray, reviewing for *The Newark Star-Ledger* Barney Collier's *Hope and Fear in Washington; the Story of the Washington Press Corps,* was divinely inspired to compose his review in the precise style of Salinger's *Catcher in the Rye,* which he had recently reread, and which I had read and despised years ago, for all its popularity. The review is a scream. It is interspersed with such gems as "big deal," "phonies," "crummy," "creepy," "puke," "the can." Here is a complete paragraph that leaves me within the legal fifty-word limit: "Anyway, when I'm finished with it all, all I really know about Dan Rather is that this Barney

Collier was once kind of in love with Rather's wife and that Eric Sevareid likes to be with his daughter and that Reston goes around calling Collier 'my boy.' "

Shall we call this a transcendental revenge (in both time and space) by a reviewer forced to read too many lousy (my adjective) books that make and hold first place on the best-seller list, and even get on high school and college required reading lists?

Vying with Collier in biting satire, but limited to book titles, is Art Buchwald, who describes an imaginary tour of a book-seller's convention at which he was introduced to the following imaginary books: *How to Perform Your Own Heart Transplant Operation; How to Make a Million Dollars in Real Estate and Have Sex at the Same Time; Releasing Inner Energy by Biting Your Fingernails; The Joy of Oil Spills; The Idi Amin Book of Etiquette; The Last Chance Food Stamp Diet Book; Dating Jackie Onassis on $5 a Day; Is There an IRS After Death?; Anita's Baby* (described as the story of a child brought up on orange juice who had a transsexual operation and won the women's singles at Wimbledon); and *Leaves* (a takeoff on *Roots*). From another source comes *The Five Million Dollar Woman*, said to be a rip-off book on Barbara Walters.

In a more serious vein comes a criticism of books that not only claim to be sexual revelations about people who are dead and can't answer or sue (Eisenhower and John Kennedy come to mind), but also on all sorts of criminals, like *The Kallinger Story* or the story of the Utah murderer who insisted on being executed. These books, says the critic, elevate prostitutes and killers to the rank of national heroes. Unfortunately, this sort of book is an ancient practice. I remember in my boyhood seeing books, interspersed with the goriest illustrations, concerning an Italian bandit chief known as *Il Passatore*, one of the most bloodthirsty scoundrels who ever existed. But at least his activities were described in terms of horror, not held up as an example to admire and imitate, like those of Jesse James and Kallinger.

More sedate is the criticism voiced by Professor Roderick Davis of John Jay College about Saul Bellow's Stockholm sermon to writers, chiding their neglect of the "fundamental, enduring, essential," and citing five literary giants who were writing after the awarding of Nobel prizes for literature began in 1901 (Tolstoy, Conrad, Lawrence, Proust, Joyce), not one of whom was honored with a Nobel prize.

Criticisms are occasionally leveled at authors for financial rather than literary practices. Alex Haley at one time sued his publisher, Doubleday, for millions of dollars in damages because Doubleday had failed to distribute enough copies of *Roots* to cash in on the acclaim for the televised version. A satisfactory compromise was reached, however, before the lawsuit came to a head. This incident reminded me of an earlier one involving my friend John Secondari, author of *(Three) Coins in the Fountain.* His publisher, Lippincott, had allowed the hardcover version of the book to run out of copies despite all the advance publicity that had been made about the forthcoming movie. But times were different then. Secondari merely shrugged his shoulders and remarked, "Oh, well, there were fortunately enough copies of the paperback to take care of the demand!" But paperbacks not only sell at a lower price than hardcovers, but the royalty percentage to the author is much lower.

A list of the ten best-sellers at seventy-five college bookstores, published in *Parade* for February 13, 1977, runs as follows:

1. *The Captains and the Kings,* by Taylor Caldwell
2. *Curtain,* by Agatha Christie
3. *Humboldt's Gift,* by Saul Bellow
4. *Roots,* by Alex Haley
5. *Passages,* by Gail Sheehy

6. *Life After Life*, by Raymond Moody
7. *The Choirboys*, by Joseph Wambaugh
8. *Against Our Will*, by Susan Brownmiller
9. *The Omen*, by David Seltzer
10. *Zen and the Art of Motorcycle Maintenance*, by Robert Pirsig

It is hard to draw any conclusion from the above list, which is quite diversified and coincides only in part with the regular best-seller list of the period. It does seem to indicate, however, that the college generations prefer books with plenty of action to those of the tranquilizing variety.

Another comparison (October 23, 1977) of the best-seller lists appearing in *The New York Times Book Review* for hardcovers and paperbacks reveals almost complete lack of coincidence between the two. For the most part difference in date of publication accounts for this. Very often when a hardcover title has been on the best-seller list, sales drop greatly when the less expensive paperback edition becomes available. For the hardcovers, we have fifteen fiction and fifteen nonfiction titles; for the paperbacks, fifteen mass market and fifteen trade titles. Out of a total of thirty titles, one only, *Your Erroneous Zones,* appears in both lists. This would seem to indicate that the markets for hardcovers and paperbacks coincide only in part at any specific time. Of this the publishers are no doubt aware, but the general public is not.

Another *Parade* item calls attention to the fact that most of our giant publishing houses form parts of vast conglomerates. Simon and Schuster, and Pocket Books, are owned by Gulf and Western Industries. CBS owns both Fawcett and Holt, Rinehart and Winston. MCA owns Putnam's. RCA has at various times owned Random House, Knopf, Pantheon, and Ballantine. Time, Inc. owns Little, Brown.

Again, the implications are doubtful. The trend, says *Parade*, is toward giant enterprises, which tend to crowd out small publishing houses. But this seems belied by the vast number of new, independent publishers who have sprouted up in recent times, particularly in California. At any rate, there is no convincing evidence that the parent company always exerts any pressure on the subsidiary publishing house, which is left free to pursue its own editorial policies, provided the latter show the all-important profit.

16 The New Sex Morality and the Generation Gap

Between the manifestations of commercialism and those of politics there is a rather large, undefined zone that shares the characteristics of both. Its branches flaunt many of the publicitarian features of commercial advertising, designed to enhance individual or group prestige, with profit motives occasionally showing. They also give rise to political movements designed to influence government and bend it to their points of view.

It is undeniable that recent years have seen a steady, progressive "liberalization" for what concerns sexuality and sexual relations, at least in the democratically run countries of the Western world and those Third World nations that are under Western cultural influence. Accordingly, we find sex, its ramifications, and its deviations far more freely discussed than was the case in the Victorian and post-Victorian eras. Prostitution existed then, perhaps to a greater extent than today, but it was largely confined to restricted red-light districts. Pornography has always existed, witness the mural paintings in the houses of Pompeii and the many pornographic works of Greek and Roman literature. Homosexuality and lesbianism were rampant then, as now. It would be easy to assert that practices fully countenanced by pagan religions went out of style, at least overtly, when Christianity, with its Judaic foundation, gained the upper hand, and that what we are now witnessing is a rebirth of paganism. The answer, unfortunately, is not that simple. Many medieval works and known practices indicate that pagan sexual "morality" (or the absence thereof) merely went underground, continuing to flourish in an atmosphere of what some would describe as hypocrisy. Is hypocrisy in these matters preferable to frankness? It has one outstanding merit: that of circumscribing the spreading by open example of practices that may be viewed as basically harmful. But the foes of hypocrisy would counter by questioning the harmfulness of such practices, and, as some do, describe them as basically beneficial.

It is a strange phenomenon that the nations that today are most conservative of the old, traditional morality are the totalitarian ones, particularly the two Communist giants, the Soviet Union and Red China. James Clarity, a *New York Times* correspondent reporting from Moscow, informs us that there is no sex education in Soviet schools, and that a country that prides itself as a world leader in social progress remains puritan in these matters. Sex discussions are seemingly taboo even in the family circle. In Red China the official policy is to discourage early courtship and early marriage, as well as all "illicit" manifestations of sexual love. Since human nature is human nature the world over, and the sexual drive is a natural instinct, it may be suspected that sex is merely driven underground there, as it was in early medieval and Victorian societies.

This is in strident contrast with what has been happening in the West and in countries under Western influence. In Japan, which never subscribed to our standards of sexual "morality," the old practices continue merrily, with some ingenious Western innovations, like the two thousand or more "love hotels" of Tokyo (their Japanese name is *abbeku,* but this is derived from French *avec,* "with," and might be expanded into "togetherness"), where unwed couples can register and dally amid lovely surroundings for periods ranging from two hours to a full week, in the best traditions of some (by no means all) of our American motels, but definitely out in the open, with no need to register as Mr. and Mrs. John Smith. Despite the French derivation of *abbeku, avec* does not appear in the appellation of the French equivalent *(hôtels de rendez-vous),* where you can spend the night, but without restaurant service, though caviar, pâté, and champagne may be served in your room.

Beginning with the noncommittal or traditional aspects of sex, the word "sexercise" was coined by a professor of medicine, Dr. Herman Hellerstein, in connection with tolerance tests conducted on heart patients, which indicate that the heart rate and blood pressure involved in sex activities are no higher than those involved in climbing a flight of stairs, with the conclusion that sex may be indulged in without danger by most people who have recovered from a heart attack.

On the thoroughly legitimate side, a marriage counselor claims sex is something you are, not something you do; a hang-up results if either the emotional or the physical angle of a relationship is carried to extremes. One is left with the impression that sexual compatibility should be ascertained before, not after, the indissoluble (?) knot is tied. But this, of course, leads us out of conventionality, and possibly into promiscuity. Betty Ford, who does not hesitate to discuss such matters frankly, at one time used the word "promiscuous" followed by a parenthetical "if the word is still in use." She is also credited with using the expression "pillow talk" (an exchange of views, not necessarily on sex, when in bed with her husband), with the added comment: "If he doesn't get it in the office in the day, he gets it in the ribs at night." The expression, however, was traced back to an earlier use by Helen Meyner, and still earlier to the title of a 1959 picture with Doris Day and Rock Hudson.

Still on the legitimate, if somewhat questionable, side is the practice current in some circles of foisting sex appeal upon girls not yet in their teens. A correspondent writes to Ann Landers about attending a party where a girl of eleven had stuffed toilet paper in her halter to make herself look as if she had a bust; but as she danced, the paper shifted, with the result that one "breast" was twice the size of the other, and on the smaller side the paper was sticking out from under her arm. Whether this was her idea or her parents', it seems to make a mockery of sex. There is no mockery, however, in the case of "nymphet," a word coined or popularized by Vladimir Nabokov in *Lolita* to describe a very young, even preteenage girl whose sexual urges are precociously developed.

Still within the legitimate field is the ever-growing institution of divorce. Latest figures show one divorce to every two or three marriages. Whatever the cause of this may be, it has given rise to a few humorous coinages. "Notice of unmarriage" announces a couple that plan to stay friends. "You are cordially invited to join us in celebrating our divorce," it goes on. There is also a comment on the fact that many people dissolve their marriages without bothering to get a divorce. The commentator wonders whether such couples should be subdivided into the "dissolutor" and the "dissolutee," and further wonders whether this "dissolution," which is the term used in some courts, has any etymological link to "dissolute."

Passing into the field of the unconventional, we come first to some fairly harmless terms, like "Eve-teaser," said to be an Indian term for "masher" or "bottom pincher"; and, on the opposite side, "The Bikinians," applied not to the inhabitants of the island of Bikini, but to a loosely organized set of wearers of the garment. (Few recall today that Bikini Island was the site of one of our earliest experiments with atomic explosions; the best bet for the semantic transfer is that when the item of apparel first made its appearance it had the effect of an atomic explosion on its viewers.)

Someone wonders whether the "tall, dark, and handsome"

male of the past generation may not now have turned into a "dirty old man," and further wonders what may be the precise difference between the old and the young of the species, outside of the age factor, and why no one ever speaks of a "dirty young man." This leads a lady who had read a columnist's admonition to a teenager that his fiftyish parents would be around "long after you've learned all you want to know about sex" to remark that no one has ever learned all he or she wants to know about sex, including herself, a grandma. Does this make her a "DOL" ("dirty old lady")? No, replies the columnist; just a "LOL" ("lusty older lady").

Elizabeth Ray has been labeled a "sexetary." But there are still a few secretaries who complain about undue advances from their male superiors, with attendant "casting-couch" setups. One such is advised to carry her complaint to the higher-ups, who may start an investigation to avoid the possible headline: SECRETARY FIRED FOR REFUSING TO LIE DOWN ON THE JOB.

NBC-TV reports that virgins are now called "squirrels" on California college campuses. Elsewhere, women who write of love affairs with politicians who are dead and can't deny it are dubbed "vaginal opportunists."

Strange terms, of which no dictionary gives a definition, occasionally crop up, like "deep kissing," though a clue is perhaps offered in *American Heritage*'s definition of "hickey": "a reddish mark on the skin caused by kissing." A girl who went on a double date where her associates wanted to "mess around" was told it was OK because the male would use his "cardigan"; but how to explain "cardigan" to her friend? The lady columnist consulted wonders what a cardigan is besides a sweater, but her daughter, perhaps more up-to-date and knowledgeable, adds that if the boy also calls the new drugstore dispenser a "condominium," she'll be better off not associating with him. There are new usages for old expressions, like "we started to *make out* on the living room sofa" (this from a fourteen-year-old girl caught in the act by her father). Ann Landers, giving some well-meant advice, ends up with "and please let me know how you make out—I mean, give me a progress report," and adds, "Boy, how the language has changed since I started to write this column!"

The French, not to be outstripped by the Americans, have set up, under the sponsorship of Health Minister Simone Veil, a "dial-a-sexpert" service (in Paris, it's 545-5646). Doctors, social workers, psychiatrists answer the calls, free of charge, and solve the sex problems, which with men are more often connected with loss of potency, and with women, to the safety of the Pill and the technique of orgasm.

That more couples are "living in sin" than ever before in our history should not be news to anyone. The Census Bureau, through two of its demographic researchers, Paul Glick and Arthur Norton, gives us approximate statistics: nearly two million adult men and women, unrelated by blood, marriage, or adoption, share the same living quarters. What they do beyond sharing is, of course, their own business. Large as the figure may seem, it represents only 2 percent of the 48 million married man-and-woman households in the nation. But this, in turn, represents an 83 percent increase since 1970 (about 523,000 as against 957,000 couples).

If it is any consolation, our 2 percent of households is surpassed by various other countries; Sweden, with 12 percent, leads the parade. Furthermore, it is not to be assumed that "sin" is at play in all these cases. Single men or women with spacious houses or apartments often take in single roomers or boarders of the opposite sex, without any romantic intention.

Nevertheless, an entire new vocabulary has arisen in connection with the problems of people who "live together" without benefit of wedlock. "Mingling" is suggested for this new way of life, based on Sylvia Porter's "mingles," for single live-togethers. But there are many other suggestions: for polite introductions, "biological companion" ("companion" alone is not bad; etymologically, it means "one you break bread with"; Latin

Americans regularly use *compañero-compañera* in the sense of a publicly recognized and acknowledged lover); "lond," from the root of "lend," combining "lover" and "friend"; "concubine," with a masculine "concubub"; "sleep-together"; "apartmate" (but "apart" might be confusing); even "son-out-law" instead of "son-in-law" and "my child's spose," rather than "spouse," implying the question "Do you *s'pose* they'll ever get married?" "Attaché" is suggested in Dr. Warren Farrell's *The Liberated Man* for a person with whom one has a deep emotional involvement, be it spouse, lover, heterosexual, homosexual, bisexual, or even asexual. There is "living friend" for a relationship that is not categorized as sexual, as in the case of two elderly persons of different sexes who cohabit to save money, as well as ordinary old-fashioned roommates of the same sex. It is further suggested that "happy nights" replace the wish "happy days" under appropriate circumstances.

Biology being what it is, some of the arrangements described above occasionally give rise to unplanned consequences. Here it is Archie Bunker who makes one of his traditionalistic pronouncements: "Bad girls get pregnant. Nice girls are expecting." Such euphemisms sound unconvincing to some members of the younger generations. One writes: "Girls don't get pregnant from 'sleeping with' guys. If all they did was sleep, there would be no pregnancy. They must have done something more!"

Yet there are others who claim that the latest wrinkle in housing arrangements is for career women to share apartments with single men. No sex; just a wholesome platonic relationship that works out well, especially for the female, because a male housemate is less nosy, more responsible, neater, and better organized than the single working woman. As for reputation, "the new morality has changed all that nonsense. No one pays attention any more. Only the squares and dried-up Puritans frown on this great set-up. And who cares what they think?" This nettles one of those Puritans, Ann Landers, who replies,

"Oh, yeah? Feed it to Sweeney! The buddies number would play, at the most, for three weeks!"

Yes, Virginia! There is a generation gap!

There is an interesting "vocabulary of seduction," supplied to Ann Landers by readers in the United States, Canada, and Mexico. They are labeled "lines," and are weasely in the extreme. Samples: "What are you afraid of? Don't be a baby. It's part of growing up"; "That's the way people express their true feelings"; "It's very painful for a guy to be in this condition and not get relief "; "It will be good for your complexion"; "Life is so uncertain! Who knows whether you will be alive tomorrow?"; "Sex is a great tension-breaker. It will make you feel relaxed"; "I want to marry you someday. Now we have to find out if we're sexually compatible"; "I've heard rumors that you're lezzie [Lesbian]. If you aren't, prove it!"; "We'll stop whenever you say"; "You have nothing to worry about. I'm sterile"; "I swear I'll never tell anybody. It will be our secret"; "It isn't sex I'm after. I'm really in love with you"; "You have the body of a woman. Nature meant for you to have sex."

All this is amusing, but hardly new. We can imagine Casanova and Don Juan voicing similar sentiments centuries ago.

Reverse pitches (from girls to boys) are few, but here is a sample, which is described as unsuccessful: "I have a terrible time with cramps every month. The doctor said I should have sexual intercourse. Help me with this medical problem!" Another, also described as a failure: "You're a goody-goody! Do you like boys better than girls?"

There is also a "vocabulary of rejection," occasioned by one of columnist Helen Bottel's correspondents, who envies her parents, in whose day no one had sex before marriage (really?), and objects to fighting off guys, then turning around and having to pretend to the girls that she is really experienced: "I'm not ready for sex"; "I'm a virgin, and I want to stay that way"; "I'm not ready for a heavy involvement."

And for a man: "I respect you too much"; "If you really care about me, you'll wait."

More serious is the matter of rape, fully publicized by such films as *Lipstick* and such books as *Against Our Will,* as well as by the charge made by a judge that many girls seem to ask for what they get by the way they dress (this cost him a recall vote and the loss of his magistracy).

There may be some truth in his assertion, though not in the case under consideration, where the girl wore blue jeans and a turtleneck sweater. A personnel officer complains of female job applicants who wear tight knit dresses unbuttoned down the front (his secretary calls it the "purl one, drop four" style; what isn't exposed you can see through the holes in the stretched knit). "Why do so many of them think they must be sexy to find work?" he plaintively concludes. The expert's reply is that perhaps they believe in the Hollywood version of the "casting couch," and urges job seekers to sell intelligence rather than availability, because relatively few of today's liberated women climb the company ladder on their backs. The problem, however, must be taken seriously. A delegation of 250 women invaded a Cleveland store to protest a display of men's knee-length socks that carried the printed message: "Help stamp out rape! Say yes!"

17 Side Issues—
Pornography and Such

One practice with a sexual angle that was much in vogue in the early 1970s was "streaking," a form of nudity in swift motion, the true motivation of which was never altogether clear. It is now very much in decline, having peaked around 1974. Its significance seems to lie somewhere between publicitarian exhibitionism (a form of personal advertising, particularly if the streaker is arrested and his or her picture gets into the papers; it cannot very well be featured on TV) and an expression of the youth protest movement, with a political base.

Nudity itself is as old as mankind. The ancients, particularly the Greeks, often carried on athletic contests in the nude. In more recent times, some cultures, by no means all primitive, have thought nothing of mixed nude bathing. Before World War II, it was customary on Japanese beaches until the government, prodded by Western visitors, decided to issue a regulation to the effect that all bathers must wear bathing suits to go into the water. The story was related to me of a retired Japanese naval officer who was seen by an American acquaintance strolling down to the beach, stark naked, but with a bathing suit slung over his shoulder. When he got to the waterline, he stopped and put it on. When his American friend expressed surprise, he replied, "The new law says we cannot go into the water unless we wear a bathing suit. Don't ask me why."

But streaking at its purest involves rapid motion as well as nakedness. Ancient Greek athletes in running competitions doubtless qualified. The first recorded occurrence of American streaking, according to the Rhode Island Historical Society, is described in an order issued by General Nathaniel Green to two Rhode Island regiments stationed on Long Island, and is dated May 18, 1776. It is to the effect that the inhabitants have complained of soldiers swimming in the nude in the mill pond, then running back to the houses naked, "with a design to insult the modesty of female decency. This scandalous conduct will be punished with the utmost severity," the general concludes.

The oldest living streaker in the United States is said to be a retired district court judge of Sacramento, California, who while at Stanford University in 1918 won a five-dollar bet by streaking down a ditch past several sorority and fraternity houses. This availed him expulsion for the remainder of the term.

By 1975 the practice was beginning to die out as the recession deepened, though a streaking centerfold of a man running at fifty miles an hour appeared in *Playgirl.* Streaking was put to double illegal use in West Germany, where five streakers, having disrobed in a bar, ran out into the street and tried to snatch women's handbags as they ran. For the record, they were caught by the vigilant West German police. Spectacular, but in long-range camera exposure, was a streaker at the Montreal Olympics. Equally striking was the appearance of a woman streaker on the New York City Center stage as the Eliot Feld Ballet danced *Cortège Parisien,* in June 1977. The audience thought at first she was one of the performers, and gasped. Then one of the dancers managed to dance her off the stage. "Take it off!" was heard at this point from some members of the audience. David Niven remarked at one Academy Awards presentation that a stripper's only applause is by stripping and showing his shortcomings.

Going back to the banner year of 1974, there was formed at New Jersey colleges a National Association of College Streakers, which rated the events by giving points based on the location of the streak and the number of students involved. At Princeton and Rutgers, streaks were held during college lectures. Another streak, involving six males, was held on the roof of the dining hall, but the streakers wore shirts, leading to their being disqualified on the ground that their exhibition was a "bottomless act," not a "pure streak," which calls for no clothes between the shoulders and the ankles; however, a scarf around the neck and a ski or Halloween mask, concealing the streaker's identity, are allowed. At Glassboro, New Jersey, one hero, clad only in a scarf, zoomed his way across campus on a motorcycle. Elsewhere, as many as seventy-five night streakers, holding sparklers, ran around the campus at night.

There was, to be sure, a reaction from the authorities. The lady mayor of Dover Township, New Jersey, for instance, set certain times of the year for permissible streaking: February 29, except in leap years, and the sixth week of March; with a penalty of one dollar for each pound of flesh exposed in streaking at any other times.

The press, ever hungry for sensationl items, collaborated by coining such alliterative phrases as "novelty of nudity" and "epidemic of epidermis," as well as "indecent exposure with intent to streak." Spectator crowds ran as high as four thousand. One streaking coed put the matter succinctly: "Streakers favor darkness. Suddenly a naked body is running at you, and just as suddenly it is gone. You don't have time to look at the face, too." And an observant columnist remarked, "One thing predictable about streakers is that they apparently always run *away* from the camera." Another, in mock morality, pronounced, "If the Good Lord had meant for us to streak, He'd have had us born naked!"

Lastly, a business firm sponsored (or permitted) on the subject of streaking an interoffice memo to all employes that read in part: "Female employes may streak on odd days, male employes on even days; all may streak on payday. Junior executives may carry their briefcases. If you streak where food is served, wear aprons. If your sex cannot be readily determined, wear a tag stating 'I am a boy' or 'I am a girl.' Secretaries may streak in their bosses' private offices only after hours or by appointment. No fig leaves; they cause skin rashes."

Somewhat akin to streaking, but more on the artistic side, is a fashion show that occurred in Vancouver, British Columbia, toward the end of 1976, featuring creations by a local designer. Midway through a dance number, a model untied the straps of her evening gown, let it drop to the floor, and danced in the nude under flashing colored lights. This delighted some TV viewers, shocked others, mainly on the grounds that children were watching the show. The producer replied that in his experience Vancouver viewers are used to this type of thing. And there the matter rested.

The issue of pornography and how to deal with it has agitated the Western world since Christianity took over from paganism. It is still a moot question whether more works of Classical literature are unavailable to us by reason of the destruction wrought by the barbarian invasions, or because of the systematic destruction of works regarded as pornographic by the early Christians. While the non-Christian world continued blissfully, and to this day, the tradition illustrated by the ancient art and literature of Egypt, India, China, and other non-Western lands, the West alternated between periods of prudery and liberalization. In recent times, Victorian standards have been replaced by the widespread acceptance of pornography in both literature and art.

A recent study conducted by two Purdue University psychologists, William Fisher and Donn Byrne, with the collaboration of thirty-one married couples who willingly subjected themselves to a battery of tests and questionnaires, concluded with the showing of a ten-minute "blue" movie depicting a man and woman making love. Those viewers who had the most negative attitudes toward sex, reporting fear, guilt, and religious proscription of sex in their upbringing, said they would favor legal restrictions against the film, and described the actors as abnormal, immoral, or bad; but they also reported the greatest increase in sexual activity during the two days following the showing. The "liberals," who described themselves as sexually uninhibited, approving of premarital sex and opposing legal restrictions on erotica, were apparently not influenced in their own behavior by the movie. The psychologists labeled the first group "eroticaphobes," the second "eroticaphiles," spoke of a possible self-fulfilling prophecy in connection with the first, and concluded that pornography can have different effects on different people. It might also be remarked that the "eroticaphiles" naturally went on doing what it was their custom to do.

There is, however, another and more harmful aspect of pornography that is discussed by Vincent Canby of *The New York Times.* He points to the escalation of acceptance of pornography in films and of the parallel escalation and acceptance of revolting scenes of violence, and of voluminous screeching in popular music. As the escalation progresses, he wonders, is there a threshold beyond which our minds, eyes, and ears get numb and no longer react to the increased stimulus? Is there a limit to the decibels, bloodshed, and lust beyond which the human being, no matter how brutal and ill-intentioned, cannot go?

On what some might describe as the beneficial side of pornographic spectacles, it was observed that during a performance of *Equus* at the University of Iowa, there was much rude and inconsiderate sneezing and coughing, but that when two of the characters took off their clothes, as required by the script, there was not even a sniffle for fully eight minutes. Has pornography healing powers?

Chief among columnists who conduct regular antipornography crusades is Jack O'Brian, creator of such terms as "The Age of Vulgarity," "showbizzy perversions," and "filth estate." He deplores the perversion of such words as "bold" to become a "sleazy euphemism for reckless cheapness"; of "mature" to reverse its meaning to signify "prurient adolescence." Even the better swear-words are ruined for special occasions, as are the "seven words you can't say on television," whatever these may be. Frank Swertlow, coining a new verb, deplores in his column what he describes as "the porning of Marie Osmond" in the 1977–1978 "Donny and Marie" series.

But other columnists are, so to speak, "pro-porn." Al Goldstein speaks of an actor having "a Barbra Streisand quality, and the most pleasurable thing to appear on the stormfront of pornography."

Obscenities appear in politics, either in the form of gestures, like Rockefeller's gestured reply to hecklers, or in actual words, such as the "screw" used by Carter in his *Playboy* article. Bill Vaughan, speaking of graffiti, says, "if there's anything more irritating than an obscene word, it's a misspelled obscene word."

"No Cover" is the title of a topless-bottomless burlesque on New York's Forty-second Street. And to prove that pornography is international, comes the title *Sinderella* from a British short animated cartoon pornographically describing the sexual exploits of traditional fairy-tale characters.

TV's serial story entitled "Soap," though watered down, drew strong criticism from the Catholic League for Religious and Civil Rights, which described it as "defamatory and tasteless" (the former because it "portrays Italian-Americans as gluttonous gangsters," the latter because its limp-wristed males and food-flinging scenes could appeal only to fifth-graders). The Southern Baptists' Christian Life Commission called it "irresponsible," "prime-time pollution," and "sex miseducation"; and a TV commentator, calling for a viewer boycott of its advertisers, urged a slogan "No Soap! to 'Soap.'"

One particularly unpleasant aspect of pornography (but this applies rather to books, magazines, and privately shown films than to TV or radio) is the featuring of sexual activities not only by teenagers but by preteenagers. A perusal of foreign newspapers and periodicals indicates that the situation is as bad in Western Europe as it is here, if not worse.

William F. Buckley defends certain aspects of court decisions dealing with pornography, such as the trial of *Deep Throat* and its producer in Memphis, Tennessee. The defendant claimed that the prosecution was unfair in selecting that city to test whether it was "obscene" by local standards. Why not select "liberal" cities, like New York or San Francisco, for a test case? It is Buckley's contention that the film in question would be found obscene even if shown in Sodom and Gomorrah, and that if Memphis is too conservative to set up standards for New York and San Francisco, then wouldn't the latter cities be too "liberal" to set up standards for Memphis?

A humorous note comes from the banning of certain books in Eldon, Missouri, on grounds of obscenity. Among the books banned from the schools was the *American Heritage Dictionary*. Why? Because it contains definitions of thirty-nine naughty words. The complainant was a Missouri highway patrolman who, according to the *Newsletter on Intellectual Freedom*, delivered himself of these immortal lines: "If people learn words like that it ought to be where you and I learned them— in the streets and in the gutters."

There can be no question about the publicitarian, profit-inspired motive of pornography and all its forms of advertising, which slip into the press media far more often than they do into TV-radio. As for the political aspects of pornography, it may be reiterated that while it is rampant in the democratic nations of the West, it is almost, if not completely, absent from the Communist countries, particularly the Soviet Union, which at the time of the Russian Revolution favored sexual freedom from "bourgeois restraints" to the point of promiscuity. So we are left with the question: "Where to draw the line between bourgeois restraints and bourgeois decadence?"

Closely related to the problem of pornography is that of prostitution, a very ancient profession, though not quite the "oldest," if one goes by the biblical account of post-Creation history. A correspondent points out to Ann Landers that before there is mention of a harlot in the Old Testament we have accounts of a tailor (Jacob), builders (Ishmael's sons), sheepherders (Abel and Laban), a housewife (Leah), a farmer (Cain), a specialist in animal husbandry (Noah's wife), and a maidservant (Hagar). This reminder leads Ann to suggest that henceforth "ladies of the evening" may be more appropriate than "members of the oldest profession." Humorous definitions (though the topic is far from humorous) are the court decision that "prostitute" cannot be used for men ("hustler" is the proper legal term), and that a client (or "john") swallows not "hook, line, and sinker," but "hooker, lie, and sinner."

There is probably no country or historical period that is free of prostitution. The difference lies in the openness with which it is carried on, and the social attitude with which the prostitute is faced. Here again, in the more democratic countries of the West, we have today a degree of social acceptance that parallels that of some past historical periods (the hetaerae of ancient Greece come to mind), while Communist lands frown upon the practice, though they may use it for their own political purposes, in the same manner that some Western business or political interests provide their clients with call girls.

We can despise the prostitute; we can pity her; we can extol her. What we apparently cannot do is abolish her as an institution.

One of the thorniest problems of our times is that of homosexuality, complicated by noisy "Gay Liberation fronts" clamoring for complete equality and openness within a basically heterosexual society; by bisexualism, even "trisexualism"; and by sex changes in individuals.

Homosexuals of both genders are numerous, well organized, and quite vocal in defense of their human and civil rights. The National Gay Task Force, which is described as including 143 organizations, recently petitioned the Federal Communications Commission to add homosexuals to the nineteen types of community groups now to be surveyed to comply with licensing renewal regulations. The "new minority" claims that 10 percent of our population, or over twenty million people, are homosexual.

It was announced early in 1977 that Gay Americans Pageants, Inc., would hold a nationwide competition to select "Miss Gay U.S.A.," "Mr. Gay U.S.A.," and "Miss Transsexual U.S.A." The competition may even be telecast.

Opposition to the official recognition of gays is at least as numerous and well organized, as proved by Anita Bryant and her followers in the Dade County, Florida, local referendum.

Again, it cannot be sufficiently stressed that the issue reaches as far back into antiquity as our records can carry us. Homosexuality and Lesbianism were rampant, with apparently little social condemnation, in Carthage, ancient Greece, and imperial Rome. Such famous names as Socrates, Sappho, and Julius Caesar come to mind. It continued, despite Christianity and prohibitions, throughout the Middle Ages and Renaissance, with an additional roster of famous names, and down into our own days, when homosexuals come openly "out of the closet," with both political and publicitarian overtones.

It has given rise to many terms, including "queen" and "gay" (the latter has been explained as stemming from a fifteenth-century custom of calling court jesters "gays"),

Other terms with weasely connotations are the psychologists' "sexual orientation," used to cover up homosexuality, and "homophobia," used to describe "irrational rage and revulsion toward homosexuals." A correspondent, claiming that sex is still popular (who would deny it?), states that now we hear about "bisexual" and "trisexual," and that "homosexual" is quite old-fashioned. Some are left wondering whether "bisexual" refers to a person who is both homo- and heterosexual, as some dictionaries claim, or to a "hermaphrodite" (one provided with both sets of sex organs), which is accepted by other dictionaries, or may be used to describe a third ancient phenomenon that has recently come into the headlines, that of change of sex after maturity, with or without the aid of surgery. (In older days, one frequently read accounts in the foreign press of girls who had been registered as boys at the time of birth, and were later called to serve in the armed forces, but had to be excused after a medical examination; but the proper dictionary term for this seems to be "transsexual.") "Trisexual" seems to have no dictionary definition. One scientific term, "gynecomastia," describes an enlargement of male breasts, which generally disappears in six months to two years, and is unrelated to either homosexuality or sex change.

As in the case of prostitution, it is easy to react to homosexuality with strong condemnation, or with ridicule, or with pity, or with noncommittal acceptance, depending on the background, religious training, and general mental attitude of the outsider.

The problem, however, presents aspects that do not lend themselves to facile solutions. Take, for instance, the case of two Lesbians, evidently persons of culture and refinement, one of whom has a young female child. How is the one who is not the mother to refer to that child, who is to her much more than "the daughter of my roommate"? She is the daughter of the person she loves, and as dear to her as though she were her own child. Ann Landers, to whom the query was addressed, wondered why the writer should feel the need to hit people over the head with the fact that she was involved in a Lesbian relationship, and somewhat flippantly suggested "the daughter of my female lover with whom I am living." But is this not displaying callousness in connection with a real human problem?

On the other side of the fence, there are writers who remind us that homosexuality exists in the "natural" world, among some animal species, notably monkeys. This is perfectly true; but they should be reminded that other phenomena exist in the natural world that the human race has relinquished as it became civilized, and now regards with strong disapproval, not to say horror: widespread aggression and wanton murder, unjustified by hunger; cruelty to the point of sadism; even cannibalism. A reversal to "nature" would plunge us back into the animal world from which some believers in evolution claim we sprang. Whether this is true or not, is such a reversal, at this stage of the game, what we want? Not even the most materialistic and godless societies would advocate it; which is not the least of their logical contradictions.

When all is said and done, certain questions remain: "What is homosexuality? A crime? If so, against whom? God? Society? One's fellow-man? Oneself? Is it a form of moral perversion, against which there are, or could be, safeguards? A psychological or physiological deviation from the norm, calling for correction? A more or less natural variant of a natural phenomenon, the sexual urge? A psychological need, like the craving for friendship and affection? A form of addiction, like alcoholism, smoking, or drugs? A mixture of all of these?" It seems as though the more homosexuals write on the subject, the less they succeed in getting across to those whose sex urges are "normal." They tell us what they do. They don't tell us why they do it. Perhaps because to them it *is* normal.

18 The Shrill Voice of Women's Lib

Historically, there is nothing new about women uniting to gain their rights, real or fancied, limited or unlimited. From ancient Greece comes the story of Lysistrata and her followers, creating an early peace movement by the unique expedient of denying themselves to husbands and lovers who preferred the exploits of Mars to the enticements of Venus. Women have led religious crusades (like Mary Baker Eddy and Aimée Semple McPherson); political upheavals (like Evita Perón and Indira Gandhi); uplift movements (like the Women's Christian Temperance Union and the suffragettes, with the constitutional amendments they sponsored). They are said to have brought on wars (like Helen of Troy and Harriet Beecher Stowe).

Women have traditionally held undisputed sway in many fields, not the least of which is the hearts of men. They are generally recognized to be healthier, longer-lived, even stronger than men. They are often more public-spirited than men (the League of Women Voters). They are wealthier than men, partly through inheritance, partly through alimony, partly through their own efforts. There is little question that they are lovelier than men (witness the many Miss America contests as against the pitifully few contests for male pulchritude). Many of them are also more assertive and aggressive, and infinitely more vocal.

Not satisfied with having achieved limited superiority, they now go after all-out equality. There are few fields in which they do not outstrip men at will (one is streaking, something they are more often afraid to do, though they don't mind disporting in bikinis). One might say that having once been forbidden to wear the pants, they prove they can be supreme without pants. In a feeble counteroffensive, men now go on display in centerfolds. Up the men! But it isn't quite the same thing.

Not all women join the Women's Liberation movement. Some are stridently vocal in their opposition. Others try to explain it, like the correspondent who claims she is subject to a psychological war going on among the "Three Me's"—the Feminine Me, sweet and girlish; the Female Me, her real gut image of herself; and the Feminist Me, her consciousness raised. The first urges her to be sweet and charming, and rely on her husband for support; the second, to work hard, save for the future, get her degree; the third, to work for the glorification of all Womankind. There is no question that all three of her Me's are thoroughly legitimate and logical.

Points of view are many and divergent. The anti-Lib movement, concentrating on stopping the passage of the Equal Rights Amendment (ERA), changes its name from "Happiness of Womanhood" to "League of Housewives." This could betoken a changed approach, but one leader says it was merely a recognition problem: some of the men who called thought "Happiness of Womanhood" was a massage parlor.

The Women's Libbers are addicted to strong language. It is reported that one leader would like to "burn anti-feminist Phyllis Schafly at the stake" for interfering with the passage of the ERA; another wanted merely to "slap" and "rough up" her opponent. Another Women's Lib advocate severely criticized Vice-President Walter Mondale for singing the praises, during the campaign, of the family, "with its authoritarian paternalistic atmosphere and its basis not on community of interest, but on blood and sex . . . in direct opposition to a nonsexist, equalitarian, democratic society." There are further strictures against "clichés and lies" that have become enshrined as "natural laws" or "commands of God."

On the other side of the spectrum is a girl who tried out for a West Point military career, then gave up. "West Point turns boys into men, but I didn't want to be turned into a man," she is quoted as saying. "I felt I was being forced to play the role of a man, being defeminized." A retired (male) Army major of sixty-one, in love with an equally retired (female) Army lieutenant colonel of fifty-five, has a problem. She insists that because she outranks him he must salute her every night before they go to bed. Perhaps the problem is authentic.

There are other problems that we can well accept as authentic. One woman objects to being referred to by her husband as "the wife" rather than as "my wife"; she is advised to refer to him as "the husband" in order to cure him. Another suggested change is that he call her "the incumbent wife," or "my first wife," but it seems to be chauvinistically jocular, as indicated by the follow-up: "It makes them try harder."

A woman office worker resents the label "the gals," by which males in the office refer to their female co-workers. Would they appreciate being referred to as "the guys," she wonders? Still another wonders why men who think nothing of using "charwoman" and "washerwoman" should gulp at "chairwoman" and "doorwoman." Also, should not the language give up such terms as "spinster" for an unmarried woman, who in this day and age seldom spins?

Not all the episodes are funny. In states that have passed ERA, and even a few that haven't, strange things can happen by reason of local laws, some because of HEW interpretations of how sexual "discrimination" is to be avoided. In South Carolina, Clover High School has traditionally crowned its homecoming queen as "Miss Blue Eagle"; this had to be discontinued because HEW decided that it is sexual discrimination to hold the contest for females only. Is the answer to add a "Mr. Blue

Eagle" contest? Not even HEW knows. There is the well-publi-cized episode of the prohibition to hold "father-son" or "moth-er-daughter" celebrations in state-supported schools.

From Sault Sainte Marie, Michigan, comes the story of a new physical education complex at Lake Superior State College that had to label its locker rooms "1," "2," and "3," instead of "Men," "Women." By general, if silent, agreement, "1" is used by women, "2" by men, and "3" is held in reserve (for bisexual individuals, perhaps?), with the proviso that if anyone objects the rooms can be rotated monthly or weekly. Elsewhere, there have been complaints about men legally going into women's rest rooms, much to the discomfort of the legitimate occupants.

Other humorous incidents include the feminist parlor game entitled "Herstory," where players roll dice and move a desig-nated number of spaces marked "Vote," "Exit from Home," "Go Home," "Go to Work," "Pay Checks," "Award Certifi-cates," etc. Men are allowed to play, and often win.

There is the story of the battle in the Iowa State Legislature over whether a new state building should be named after An-selm Briggs, first governor of the state, or after Carrie Chapman Catt, a leader in the struggle to grant women the vote. This was opposed by male chauvinist pig legislators, who objected that people would start calling the new building the "Catt House."

One correspondent inquires whether the Hispanic *macho* can be interpreted as the equivalent of "male chauvinist pig." (Yes and no.) Another asks whether Women's Lib contemplates inaugurating a National Men-Watching Week to balance the Girl-Watching Week that is unofficially in effect in some locali-ties (why not?). A third states that a woman came to her door and introduced herself as "Your Fuller Brush Man," and won-ders whether soon a man will ring and say, "I'm your Avon Lady." (By all means!)

One of Helen Bottel's correspondents complains about her husband, who in recent times had become kingly and violent, insisting she should both work on the outside and do all the housework, said she made him feel trapped, and finally left her in the middle of the night. He had not been seen or heard from for ten days. What should she do? "Give three rousing cheers!" was the reply. This reminds me of a reverse experience when I was an assistant in the Italian consular agency in Albany, New York, many years ago. The consular agent was a kindly, cultured man with a long white beard, to whom the local Italians working on the railroad came for advice on all sorts of problems. One came in one day and told the agent, "On the day of the feast of Saint Anthony my wife ran away, and I haven't heard from her since. What should I do?" Dr. Baccelli smiled benignly, stroked his beard, and replied, "My boy, go light a candle to Saint Anthony, to whose intercession with God you owe this favor from Heaven."

But some problems are not so easily solved. An assistant principal in Morristown, New Jersey, complains about coed physical education, which is far from a panacea in his eyes. The local paper had shown boys and girls playing softball together. Of course, the boys, who play other boys' teams, enjoy "jazzing around" with the girls in a picnic atmosphere, he says. But when a girl breaks her arm competing against boys in a noncontact sport, or is unable to react quickly enough to avoid injury, is that really ensuring equal opportunity?

Some states, like Oklahoma, have been forced to repeal local laws setting age twenty-one for men, as against eighteen for women, for the purchase of beer. After all, equality is equality. But from England comes a strange request for equality. In Leicester, girls are demanding equal rights to be caned (yes, caned!) with the boys. A mixed party of seventeen-year-olds was discovered drinking at a local bar. The boys were caned by the headmaster, but the girls only had privileges for older pupils withdrawn. The girls were furious and complained, "We should all have been caned!" But the education department was unimpressed, and refused to change its evil, discriminatory ways.

One thing that has always gotten on my nerves is the radio

ad for a bank that offers services of various kinds to its clients. "Your Anchor banker—he understands!" is invariably followed by a feminine voice: "Your Anchor banker—*she* understands!" Actually, in the banks I deal with, the absolute majority of all employees are women. Perhaps they should leave just "she" in the ad. Another source of irritation to me is a printed ad about meat cuts that are featured not on a side of beef, but on a woman's body. Perhaps Women's Lib should attend to that. Or perhaps it already has; I haven't seen the ad for a while.

As against all this, there is an episode of old-fashioned chivalry. Trish Reilly, loveliest of CBS's news reporters at the time she was there, appeared one day from a field of winter sports, chicly arrayed in a complete set of snow togs. "I'll have to buy a snowmobile to match!" she remarked to the coach. "It would look pretty with you!" he gallantly replied.

Is there a legitimate and just angle to the Women's Lib movement? Of course there is, particularly on the legal side, which is translated into political action. It has been abundantly proved that women are often discriminated against in matters of employment, compensation, and civil rights, and it is high time these injustices were remedied, through the legal-political machinery provided by our democratic form of government.

Between two applicants with equal qualifications, many employers prefer the man to the woman. Sometimes this preference is justified by the nature of the work to be performed; just as often it is not. This situation is not properly rectified, however, by decreeing that all women are equally qualified with all men for active police or firefighting duty, for combat duty in the armed forces, for professional football. There may be exceptional cases, and these should be considered on an individual basis. Duly qualified women employees are often passed over in the matter of promotions. These cases, too, call for individual consideration rather than blanket bureaucratic decisions. There is no question that women are entitled to equal pay for equal work, regardless of whether they are married or single, with or without dependents. If they can produce the proper qualifications, they should by all means be entitled to equality in the issuance of credit cards, the signing of contracts or leases. On the other hand, true equality requires that they should assume equal obligations and responsibilities in matters of alimony and child support where they are gainfully employed and their divorced partners are not.

Also, abundant provision should be made for women who do not care for full equality, and prefer the status quo. A woman who wishes to be a housewife and mother, attend to all the traditional occupations associated with that status, and rely for support on her husband should have untrammeled freedom to do so, and not be regarded with scorn by her Women's Lib sisters. If necessary, some basic conditions could be laid out in a marriage agreement worked out in advance.

When all is said and done, there is enough constructive work laid out for an intelligent Women's Lib movement to warrant the abandonment of the more grotesque and laughable features that have been fastened upon by the media because they are sensational and attention-getting.

A full generation ago, George Bernard Shaw, after remarking that fascinating women do not care for emancipation because they know that they can govern through their dominance of men, went on to conclude, "It is only the proud, straightforward women who wish, not to govern, but to be free."

Women's Lib groups are numerous, well organized, and active in many countries besides ours. As is natural, each national movement has its own cultural characteristics. A sample is Japan's feminist movement, reported at length by Paul Raffaele in *Parade*. Founded by a thirty-two-year-old housewife, Misako Enoki, it was first officially known as the Chupiren Association, unofficially as the "Pink Panthers," by reason of the pink helmets bearing the feminine biological symbol that the members wore. Before their appearance, Japan was one of the worst offenders in the matter of women's rights. If employed, women were paid less than half of what men received for similar work, and were subject to sudden divorce with little or no alimony at a husband's whim. Chupiren achieved substantial gains in both fields during its rather brief existence, mainly through noisy demonstrations and publicity, directed particularly at sinning husbands. But when it became a political party and fielded ten candidates for Japan's Upper House, all were defeated. Mrs. Enoki, who had borrowed heavily to finance the political campaign, had also sworn that if defeated she would either divorce her husband or repay her debt by dissolving her organization and working for her husband. She chose the latter course. The husband's reaction? *"Ano ne!"* ("Well, well!" or "You don't say!") Was he pleased or sorry? No one knows, for the Japanese can be inscrutable if they want to.

19 Women's Lib and the Common Tongue

Turning to the purely linguistic aspects of the Women's Liberation movement in recent times, some of the developments show features of the episodic variety, others deserve careful attention by reason of their possible impingement upon the language of the future. They also bear comparison with what goes on in other languages.

One item of general interest is the question of whether and how women's speech differs from men's. Is it, as some have asserted, "emotional, vague, euphemistic, sweetly proper, mindless, endless, high-pitched, silly"? Even the great linguist Otto Jespersen, back in 1922, stated that "women frequently leave sentences unfinished, and are prone to jump from one idea to another when talking," which if true, is bad; and that they have "an instinctive shrinking from coarse and gross expressions," which if true, would be good. But a number of present-day coeds interviewed on the subject tended to respond with an expletive to be deleted. Another criticism of the earlier period was to the effect that women used more adjectives and -*ly* adverbs ("nicely," "terribly," "sweetly," etc.). But a recent study conducted at the University of Illinois by Professor Cheris Kramer would seem to indicate that either the charges were unfounded at the time they were made or that the feminine speaking and writing style has changed radically in the course of the last half century. Professor Kramer reports that there is no significant difference in any of the sectors mentioned above. Interesting, if true. My own impression is that a difference is still perceptible, particularly in the case of women of the over-thirty generations. On the other hand, certain once feminine expressions and combinations (like *"So* lovely!") tend to be taken over by men. Another observation I have made is that women are at least as prone as men to create and spread innovations in vocabulary. Perhaps a more comprehensive survey would bring additional facts to light.

More basic, perhaps, from the standpoint of Women's Lib, is the question: "Does a sexist language exist?"; or, even more basically: "Is our language intrinsically sexist?"

Individual complaints about sexist language are legion. One correspondent wonders why a tough male manager is called a "hard taskmaster," but a woman in the same position "hard to work for"; why he "makes a quick decision," while she is "impulsive"; why, if he reacts strongly, he is being "only human," while she is described as "emotional." In other situations, he is "decisive," she is "stubborn"; he is a "man of the world," she has "been around."

When someone suggested that "domestic engineer" replace "housewife" in our vocabulary, someone else ironically suggested "doctor of domestic drudgery" as a more suitable replacement; another, versed in the Classics, "oikologist" (specialist in the home). To another complaint that a divorced man goes back to being a "bachelor," while the woman is a "divorcée" ("spinster" was laughed to scorn), columnist Helen Bottel suggested "dingle" for a divorced person.

Writer Janet Lowe objects to the categorization of books as "women's literature," and looks forward to the day when we shall all be reading about the exploits of a female advertising wizard in a book titled "The Gray Flannel Pantsuit," or a political portrait of "Ms. President," or a thriller about "How the Good Girls Finally Won."

But all this is not getting down to the core of the matter. Trust the bureaucrats to implement women's desire for full equality with provisions that have the force of laws. Australia has officially decided to give up the questionable practice of giving hurricanes and cyclones feminine names. In deference to the UN International Women's Year, the Australian Bureau of Meteorology decided to use both male and female names. This, incidentally, brought out a historical curio. The practice of naming cyclones started some eighty years ago, and at first the names used were those of Australian politicians. The politicians complained, and the bureau switched over to the names of the politicians' wives, then to women's names generally. The practice became worldwide. In America, feminine names for hurricanes persist, despite a feminist's suggestion that perhaps they should be replaced by names of senators, "who love to have things named after them." One feminine name recently added to the list is "Babe"; but wasn't that the nickname of a very masculine home-run king, "Babe" Ruth?

But our own bureaucrats have to be on the job in other areas. The 1976 Department of Labor's *Dictionary of Occupational Titles* shows extensive changes designed to rid the language of sexism. "Custom sewer" now replaces both "seamstress" and "dressmaker," despite the possibility of mispronouncing the second word in the combination, plus the fact that "dressmaker" is noncommittal. "Busboys" are now "dining-room attendants," thus avoiding both "busgirl" and "buswoman." The former "governess" is now a "child mentor," and a "maid" has become a "houseworker." The former "takeoff man" and "takeoff girl," whatever the terms may mean, are now "battery plate remover" and "form stripper," respectively (the second sounds provocative, but no matter). Jack Smith, who has researched the topic for the *Los Angeles Times,* concludes by praising England, whose citizens are brought up not by "child mentors," but by nannies.

The New York State Department of Education, in a report on "Reviewing Curriculum for Sexism," advocates the following replacements in textbooks: "humanity" for "mankind," "artificial" for "man-made," "leader" for "statesman," "husband and wife" for "man and wife." "Women," says the report, "should be spoken of as participants in the action, not as possessions of the men." Thus, phrases like "Pioneers moved west, taking their wives and children with them" and "Jim Weiss allows his wife to work part-time" are tabooed.

In the matter of revising school texts, it is reported from California that a textbook company was trying to sell to the authorities a children's arithmetic textbook with illustrations. One of these represented elephants doing a ballet. The elephants all wore tutus, which marked them as feminine. These had to be removed, on the ground that "the tutus would impair the development of the proper self-image among female pupils." One wonders why, since the ballet normally features more female than male dancers, and is one of the leading performing arts.

In the case of another textbook, a picture showing mother bringing sandwiches to dad as he fixes the roof is banned. In still another, a picture of dad lugging in a heavy basket of tomatoes while ma and daughter, in pretty dresses and aprons, are working at the kitchen table had to be reversed in a revised edition. Mother and daughter now lug in the tomatoes while dad and son are at the kitchen sink. This is the concept of "unisex," which is far from having universal acceptance.

A charge of sexism, rather surprisingly, is leveled at the TV industry by the United States Commission on Civil Rights, which accuses the networks of portraying women and minorities as stereotypes and of discriminating against them in employment. According to the report, white males dominate TV drama, appearing in over 65 percent of all roles, and appearing more frequently in serious roles, as well as portraying older, more independent characters having diverse and prestigious occupations, while white females have less than 24 percent of all roles, many of them comic. This situation is not at all evident to the casual, or even habitual, TV viewer, save perhaps in programs dealing with crimes and police activities. It might have been more to the point to deplore the glamorization of women in many programs.

In the religious field, Dr. Nathan Wright offers a replacement for parts of the Bible and the Doxology: "Father of our Parents" for "Father of our Fathers," and a reference to the Jewish maiden as being "overshadowed" rather than inseminated by the ghostly manifestation of an obviously male God. He would rewrite the Doxology verse that reads: "Praise God from Whom all blessings flow/Praise Him all creatures here below/Praise Him above, ye heavenly host/Praise Father, Son and Holy Ghost" to read as follows: "The God to Whom all life belongs/-Let praise be given in endless song/Let Heaven shout, Earth join the praise/of God Who blesses all our days." The versification is certainly on a par with the original, and God, a pure spirit, is presented as sexless. Anyone contrary-minded?

It being fashionable these days to compose new, up-to-date versions of the Bible, it is not surprising that the new edition of the Revised Standard Version makes concessions to the feminist movement. It was announced in June 1977 that for Matthew 22:13 the committee favored a change from "there men will weep and gnash their teeth" to "weeping will there be, and gnashing of teeth." In Romans 5:7, for "one will hardly die for a righteous man," the committee favor "for someone who is righteous." Where the First Psalm reads "Blessed is the man who walks not in the counsel of the wicked," the new edition may read "Blessed are those who walk not."

Not to be outdone, Reform Judaism, in its new book for home prayer, has replaced the traditional "God of our Fathers" with "God of all generations." There is also a new "Covenant of Life" prayer that initiates girls into the congregation when they are eight days old, a ceremony previously reserved for boys only.

Not the least of the legitimate aims of Women's Lib has to do with forms of address. One such that is peculiar to American English usage is that of labelling a married couple "the John Smiths," or "Mr. and Mrs. John Smith," and referring to the female partner as "Mrs. John Smith," as though she had given up not only her family name, but even her first and feminine name by reason of the accident of marriage. This unique custom is occasionally not justified, but defended on the ground that it conventionally indicates that "Mrs. John Smith" is still happily married or is widowed, while "Mrs. Mary Smith" indicates that she is divorced. In addition to being slightly ridiculous, this explanation blankets the fact that the woman's right to separate individuality is being violated, regardless of what books of etiquette may say. In addition, it has no parallel in the Western world. Some languages, like Spanish, make provision for the women to retain even her original family name as a full part of her married identity (Señora Luisa Gutiérrez de González indicates that she, originally Señorita Luisa Gutiérrez, married into the González family. In Italian, Luisa Ferri Pei, though less often used, indicates that Luisa Ferri married into the Pei family). At any rate, no Western language save English deprives a woman of her first name and imposes that of her husband upon her.

Two additional, quite legitimate complaints are voiced. A man is asked for his "surname"; why should a woman be asked for her "maiden name"? Then there is that legalistic horror, appearing in documents and deeds: "John Doe et ux." (this is an abbreviation for Latin *et uxor,* "and wife"). Legally speaking, says Barbara Freedman, does this imply that she is automatically interchangeable with any other female who comes along? She goes on to speculate that someday, in the case of couples that are not legally married but own joint property, we could

have "John Doe et amica" ("and [woman] friend"), or, in the
case of homosexual couples, even "John Doe et amicus" ("and
[man] friend"). And if the wife is working and the husband is
not, could we have "Jane Doe et maritus" ("and husband")?

There is more support, logically and linguistically, even
among women, for the retention of the distinction between
"Miss" and "Mrs." It must, however, be admitted that the use
of "Ms.," particularly in correspondence (in speech, "Miz"
sounds a bit regional), is a great help in solving doubts when
writing to a woman whose married status you don't know. Some
object that the use of "Ms." identifies the writer as pro-Women's
Lib; I find myself gratefully using it under the appropriate circumstances of ignorance.

An added angle is confusion of sex, where the first name is
ambivalent (Jody, Lynn, Marion, etc.). For this, the written title
"Mx." (pronounced "Mix"?) is suggested, contrasted with "Mr."
But it is still noncommittal as to the lady's conjugal status, if
Lynn turns out to be a woman. The claim has been advanced
that "Ms." stands for "Marxian sister," but for this there is no
foundation. "Ms." has been traced all the way back to 1825. The
other objection, that "Mrs." is an abbreviation of "mistress,"
and that the latter has a possible double meaning, does not hold
much water, in view of the present-day difference between the
two forms, both in spelling and pronunciation.

The question of titles to be used in connection with the two
sexes lends itself to some considerations of international usage.
In English, "doctor" and "professor" are used for members of
both sexes, despite the existence of feminine suffixes that are
used in other connections ("actor-actress," "waiter-waitress,"
etc.). The same word holds true for both sexes with "ambassa-
dor," usually "minister," and other exalted occupational titles,
as far down as "teacher" (not, however, for titles of nobility,
which are established by ancient tradition ("king-queen," "sir-

dame," "lord-lady," "count-countess," etc.). In the Romance languages there are usually feminine forms (Spanish *doctora, profesora;* Italian *dottoressa, professoressa, ambasciatrice,* but not yet *ministra;* French offers an occasional *doctoresse,* but for the most part uses the masculine form with *femme* prefixed if required for clarity). German, despite the availability of a feminine suffix like *-in* (used, however, in *Lehrerin,* a woman teacher), uses masculine forms. The prefixing of *Frau* indicates not a professional woman, but the wife of a professional man. Russian, despite an absolute majority of women doctors in the Soviet Union and the abundant availability of feminine suffixes and endings, uses masculine forms for both sexes, thereby presumably branding itself as hopelessly sexist.

Very recently there arose a controversy in America over "esquire," often used in written forms of address to lawyers. Some lawyers argued in the pages of the *New York Law Journal* that the title originally referred to a knight's attendant or a member of the English landed gentry, and should apply only to men. Others were in favor of making it ambivalent, while one came up with an archaic and somewhat suspect "esquiress."

The suffix *-ess* is only one of many that appear in English to distinguish between the two sexes, and its use is demanded by some women (Michele Phillips, for instance, resents actors and actresses being lumped together under "actors." "Hopefully," she says, "I will be known as an actress, but never as an actor"). Another actress, Jacqueline Bisset, is quoted to the effect that "housewife" is still "housewife" in Italian, not "family engineer"; that in England a female committee chief is still "chairman," not "chairperson"; that in French the suffix *-ette* is immutable. We might add that *-ette* is abundantly used, even overused, in English as well: "drum majorette" is well known; a girls' team from Buffalo described itself as the "Buffalettes"; while "astronette" is suggested for a lady astronaut. Even "coppette" has been heard for feminine members of the police.

Prefixes, too, come in for an inning. In Paparazzi, a New York City pub on Second Avenue, the rest rooms are labeled "PAPArazzi" and "MAMArazzi."

Where the English language seems to experience a real need is in the matter of singular personal pronouns: "he," "she"; "his," "her" or "hers"; "him," "her." Note, in contrast, the delightfully noncommittal "they," "their," "theirs," "them" in the plural, which can be masculine, feminine, or inclusive of both. How often have we regretted the necessity of saying "he or she," "his or her"? Numerous suggestions have been voiced for a set of personal pronouns that would be not neuter or sexless, like "it," "its," but of common gender. Don Rickter, a pioneer in the field of sex-language reform, reminds us that *Time* magazine of March 20, 1972, listed three definite possibilities: "ve," "ver," "vis"; "te," "tem," "ter"; and "co," "co," "cos"; while *United Nations World* of May 1, 1973, offered "xe," "xen," "xes" (pronounced *zee, zen, zes*). "A person gets what te deserves" clearly sounds better, and is more economical of time and space, than "a person gets what he or she deserves". This is reminiscent of languages like Chinese, Japanese, or Hungarian, which do not carry the notion of sex into their grammatical structure (*ön* in Hungarian can mean either "he" or "she," just as "they" in English can refer to a group of all women, all men, or a combination of the two). Unfortunately, these useful suggestions do not seem to take hold.

The Women's Lib form that has definitely caught on, though mainly for purposes of satirization, is "person." Its use to replace "man" (or "woman," for that matter) is occasionally useful. A Canadian Tourist Office circular, for example, makes its appeal, among others, to "fisherpersons," recognizing the fact that there are fisherwomen as well as fishermen. A help-wanted ad for a "waitperson" is intended to signify that either a waiter or a waitress may apply. More often, however, "person" clouds the issue. Since the sex of the "chairperson" is normally known, is it advantageous to use that word instead of "chairman" or "chairwoman"? Is "personhood" (which can be legitimately used, in the sense of "individuality") a suitable replacement for either "manhood" or "womanhood"? Or "personfully" for "manfully" or "womanfully"?

Some of the seemingly serious examples make one wonder whether there is, in effect, a conspiracy to cast ridicule upon the use of "person." The director of New York's Harris Gallery, for instance, speaks of a "caveperson doodling an antelope on a wall in the Dordogne." The Iowa Department of Social Service speaks of a telephone number that was to be "personed" twenty-four hours a day (of double interest is the functional shift of "person" from noun to verb, on the analogy of "man," "to man," leading the reporter to suggest: "Person the battle stations, male chauvinists!"). Then we run into "freshperson power" for the colleges (this neatly avoids "freshman"; but has "freshwoman" been put to use; or might it be misunderstood?). A Michigan school-funding bill provides programs for "pregnant persons." Medically speaking, says the editor, this is an idea that deserves to expire after a "pregnant pause."

Deliberate and malicious satire begins with "The Siblinghood of Personkind" ("Brotherhood of Man"), attributed to Thomas Middleton, and continues all the way to a full article, "And God Created Person," by Professor Merrell Clubb of the University of Montana, published in *Modern Language Association Newsletter* for March 1974, which, starting mildly enough with "chairperson," "policeperson," and the like, goes on to remove "man" and affix "person" to the following (try it out for yourself): country, kins, longshore, fore, post, brake, milk; then prefixes "person" to hunt, slaughter, hole, liness, -of-war; and, as a climax, room. But he also suggests a remedy: prefix "wo-" to "person" ("wopersonsroom"). This "wo-" prefix will also be of signal help in the case of power, lib, of the house; but it does reintroduce the sex distinction. After a disquisition on the etymology of good old Anglo-Saxon "man" and "woman," in contrast to Johnny-come-lately, French-based "person," he goes on to suggest suitable revisions for some literary titles of note: *Two Gentlepersons of Verona, Essay on Person, Person and Superperson, The Iceperson Cometh.* Even for such an institution as Bemelman's Bar, the suggestion "Bemelperson's Bar" has been advanced, albeit facetiously.

Another writer, in *Harper's Weekly,* would delete "man" and use "person" in a long list of words: mansion, Manhattan, management, mania, Manx, mandolin, manicure, permanent, manipulate, mantilla, maneuver, manner, and Mansfield (Ohio). But that's going a bit out of the way.

An alternative for "person" in connection with "hench" was suggested in an article on feminine crime: "henchwomen," with "henchpersons" where the sexes mingle their criminality. Another, in connection with those legislators (a few were women) who abetted Governor Brendan Byrne of New Jersey in obtaining passage of his state income tax against the will of the people, was "henchpeople."

A coinage of an entirely different variety, designed to keep the sexes apart, appears in the *House Judiciary Proceedings* of 1974: "the gentlelady from New York" (the reference is presumably to Bella Abzug). The record does not indicate whether she was pleased.

Reluctantly parting with linguistic aspects, it must be noted that women who like to invade men's premises are not always prepared to grant men the same privilege. Though many of their members had more or less forced their way into boys' baseball Little Leagues, the Girl Scouts firmly rejected the idea of accepting boys into their midst, on the ground that it would "cramp their style," something that can readily be granted. It would do them good, however, to look up the etymology of "girl"; in origin, it referred to the young of either sex, and is so used in a few isolated English and Scots dialects even today.

A more melancholy item is to the effect that sex differences have been effaced among teenagers in the matter of smoking and drinking, according to a recent study that included both high schools and junior high schools. Today, the average number of intoxications for both boys and girls is five times a year. Ten years ago, boys got drunk twice as much as girls; the boys haven't gone down; the girls have come up. Not even the most ardent Women's Libber would claim that this is an improvement, however much it may equalize the sexes.

One anti-Libber protests the appropriation by Congress of five million dollars for the holding of International Women's Year conferences. She charges that the program of activities is custom-tailored to favor lobbying for pet programs of the Libbers: Lesbian marriages, sexual integration in sports, wages for housewives, abortion, the Equal Rights Amendment, free day-care programs. All this while in many states food programs for the elderly and incapacitated are being cut back, along with help for the retarded and handicapped.

One final note deals with the psychological problems of "reentry" into the working world of women who have long been home-bound. According to some psychologists, they are subject to the same anxieties that beset them when they first entered the working world fifteen or twenty years earlier: fear of inadequacy, of self-assertion, of young male co-workers who may regard them as a threat to their own advancement, even conflicts between the woman's sense of personal and professional identity. Whether this is a peculiarly feminine problem rather than a personal one may, however, be questioned. Men, too, have been known to go to pieces when reentering, after an absence of many years, an occupation or field of activity with which they were once familiar.

One disquieting factor from the standpoint of the Women's Lib movement is a survey conducted by *Family Planning Perspectives*, the journal of Planned Parenthood, based on a representative sample of nearly 7,000 married women between ages fifteen and forty-four. The report, released in November 1977, shows that 49 percent of the respondents had a preference for male offspring, while only 32 percent preferred girls; 19 percent preferred an equal number of both sexes. The trend in favor of male offspring was more pronounced among women under thirty than in the thirty-one-to-forty-four group.

Why the bias in favor of new male chauvinists on the part of women? Factors of education, income, race, religion, region, urban versus rural areas made no significant difference. "Cultural forces," it was suggested, were at work. What kind of cultural forces? The report didn't say. Natural attraction of one sex for the other? The tacit thought that a male child would have a better chance than a girl of making his way in the world? An equally unspoken, subconscious recognition of male superiority by the female respondents?

It might be interesting to carry the survey further, and poll an equal number of married men as to their preferences. It would be equally interesting to ask both men and women direct questions: "Why, if you had three children, would you rather have two boys and a girl than two girls and a boy?" "Why would you prefer your firstborn to be a boy (or a girl)?" The answers might be enlightening to and concern the Women's Liberation movement.

20 The Young, the Old, the In-Between

There are various ways of subdividing and classifying people —by race, nationality, religion, sex, age group. Each classification is legitimate. Each has its own special language, or at least vocabulary and semantics. Each is subject to the two forces of which the media are the carriers: political indoctrination and commercial propaganda.

If we subdivide humanity by age groups, the most common headings are children, teenagers, young adults, mature adults, elderly people. Each group to some extent merges into the next, but each has its own individuality and problems.

Children (from birth to twelve) are much in the news; but as a rule they are passive recipients rather than actively conscious agents. Their recipient role is particularly manifested in their home training, what they get in the schools and in the streets, and, above all, what they get out of the media—TV, radio, comic books and strips, occasionally even school texts. There is what might be described as "Children Power"; but it is largely manufactured for the children by outside agencies inspired by self-interest (occasionally by genuine concern, as when medicine containers are deliberately made difficult to open, and matches in a book made difficult to pull out for use; both these practices can be irritating to adults, but their intention to protect children from accidental poisoning or burning has to be acknowledged).

There is also a child language, highly unstable and fluctuating, which tends to imitate and merge with that of the next age group, and is strongly influenced by the media.

Teenagers (thirteen to nineteen), having achieved maturity of sorts, are far more originally creative, both in ideas and language. They, too, however, are strongly influenced by the propaganda media, which spread their own as well as the teenagers' innovations.

The young adults (twenty to forty) and the more mature adults (forty-one to sixty) are more reflective and practical in their outlook. Here the amount of influence exerted by the media depends in large part on the cultural and educational background of the individual, social status, occupation, labor union affiliation, etc.

Senior citizens (sixty-one on) are keenly conscious of retirement problems. They are strongly influenced by media propaganda purporting to cater to their interests. But they are also mature and conscious enough to act on their own behalf. Senior (or "Gray") Power is something that both advertisers and politicians know they have to reckon with.

Of all our groups, the most politically active until recently were the teenagers, joined in special situations, such as the Vietnam War, by the younger adults concerned with draft status; and the senior citizens, spurred by the problem of survival in a world that no longer needs them.

Younger children are seldom propagandized along political lines, but much sought after for commercial purposes. To some extent, the influence of schools and sound programs like "Sesame Street" is canceled out on TV by scenes of violence (even cartooned ones, like the "Hawaiian Punch") and by deliberate misspelling of brand names and words associated with them. (It is an ancient joke that a whole row of school spellers went down on "does," which they insisted on spelling DUZ.) The more recent counterpart is the spelling of "We are" as "We R," on the analogy of the brand slogan "Toys R Us."

There is the constant spreading of such elegant interjections as "wow!" (surprise, pleasure, enthusiasm); "yuk!" (dislike, disgust, disapproval); "whammy!"; "zinggo!"; "klunk!"; etc. There are names of foods, such as broccoli and spinach, that the kiddies consider obscene enough to scribble on walls and blackboards. There are other words that, according to Erma Bombeck, have to be censored out of children's programs because reaction to them is violent ("work," "walk," "go to bed"). There are jokes like the one about a boy who remarks to his dad, poring over a report card, "Of course I seem stupid to my teacher! After all, she's a college grad!"; or the one about dad's reply to the boy's query "What does it mean to be college-bred?": "That's a four-year loaf made from the flower of youth and his old man's bread."

One potentially distressing phenomenon is reported in a partial survey conducted by *The Christian Science Monitor* (November 15, 1976). It indicates that young children are held and fascinated by commercials far more than by regular programs. Their eyes brighten up and their attention becomes fixed when the commercial comes on, which is, as a norm, the opposite of what happens with older viewers. Is this the shape of the brainwashed to come?

Both younger children and teenagers are described as being strongly influenced by violence on TV. In the case of the former, a survey conducted by the Foundation for Child Development indicates a mixture of fascination and fear. The fear was most noticeable in children who spent four or more hours a day watching TV programs. Some were afraid that "somebody bad might get into my house"; others were afraid to go out. The objects of their fears were specific figures in their neighborhoods (30 percent), their own fathers (10 percent), imaginary characters, like the Devil or the Frankenstein monster (15 per-

cent). Other TV influences on preteenagers included their naming popular entertainers and athletes as famous persons (Cher,
Marie Osmond, Elvis Presley, O. J. Simpson, Muhammad Ali),
with fewer than 2 percent picking American political figures,
usually George Washington or Abraham Lincoln, and only 1
percent humanitarian figures, mostly Florence Nightingale.

The reaction of teenagers, more specifically high-school students, was characterized by resentment rather than fear. In a
poll of 18,000 such students conducted by *Scholastic Magazine,*
66 percent held that juveniles who commit acts of violence
should be treated as adult criminals, with only 20 percent opposing.

As the children's language merges with the teenagers', we
get a broad expansion of the "wow!" used as a general expression of enthusiasm; the new use of "ape" where the older generation would have used "crazy" ("I'm ape over Shirley"); the use
of "sex fiend" as a compliment ("Mommy, is daddy a sex
fiend?"), and of "cool" where the older generation would have
used "hot"; of "brown-nosing" (laughing hysterically at
teacher's dumb jokes); of implications of rebellion for its own
sake ("If my parents like this, can I return it?"). There is a
spreading use of clichés ("No way!"; "That's a good question!";
"So what else is new?"; "I thought you'd never ask!"). These
replace such older ones as "You don't say so!" and are pregnant
with semantic overtones meaningful to native speakers; compare "You don't say so!" with Spanish *"Hombre! No me digas!"*
or French *"Sans blague!"* "Meaningful" itself has turned into a
cliché, especially in connection with "relationship"; so has
"coming to grips with reality," or "to find yourself."

Then there are the specifically teenage programs on TV, with
their own creations, which are, of course, spread by word of
mouth ("Sweathogs," "Get bent!," "Up your nose with a rubber
hose!," all from "Welcome Back, Kotter"; or Fonzie, the teenage superman with 150 girl friends, who is tough and makes

adults look silly and stupid (this seems to be the modern analogy to *Catcher in the Rye*, which gained wide acceptance among the younger generations, and even in the schools).

The generation gap in language is fully illustrated by such stories as dad's reference to Rudy Vallee as a singer who used a megaphone ("Dad, what's a megaphone?"), or to "I Found a Million-Dollar Baby in a Five-and-Ten-Cent Store" ("What's a five-and-ten-cent store?").

Language is forever changing. Fortunately, the teenage language changes fastest and most drastically of all. The expressions listed above will probably be dead and buried inside of ten years. In the meantime, they clutter up the landscape and are enthusiastically touted by the media.

The political teenage language of the Vietnam War has already largely disappeared. The biggest casualty is the use of "pigs" to refer to law-enforcement agents ("Smoky Bear" is far more endearing). Its only large-scale survival is in "male chauvinist pig," a Women's Lib expression, but even that is being satirized out of existence.

There is today among college students widespread acceptance of the practice of leaving college after one or two years, going into the outside world, either to work or to tour the country, then going back to their studies fortified, we hope, by their practical experiences. This is known as "taking a breather" for the purpose of "finding oneself." The slogan, supplied by Reverend Timothy Healy, president of Georgetown University: "There is nothing sacred about four years!"

For the language of the mature adults, a correspondent, combining age and sex, offers a somewhat different classification from mine: up to eleven, "boys and girls"; twelve to sixteen, "kids and gals"; seventeen to thirty-five, "guys and ladies" (what about "dolls"?); from thirty-five on, "men and women"; no provision for senior citizens, but see below. It is objected by another correspondent that "guy" is often used in the feminine

("She's a nice guy"; "Hey, you guys!" in programs like "Charlie's Angels"). Others feel that "gals" is a bit disrespectful.

A mature-age problem of a different order is posed by columnist William F. Buckley. When is it appropriate to shift from addressing someone as "Mr." (or "Senator," or "Governor") So-and-So to using the first name? When this is done on first acquaintance, he labels it an "obsessive egalitarian familiarity which approaches a raid on someone's privacy." Would you call Socrates "Soc"? Would you address the President as "Jimmy"? (It has been done!) Being "one of the boys" (or "girls," as the case may be) comes easy enough when you are in college, but in later years? It would seem, however, that the problem can be rather easily solved by common agreement.

The trouble is that after the common agreement come memory lapses. The person you are trying to train yourself to call Bill comes out, to his surprise, as "Mr. Buckley," and he wonders if your friendship is cooling. Speakers of languages that make a distinction between a familiar and a polite form of address (and they are an absolute majority) have a far graver problem. You have agreed to *tutear,* or *tutoyer,* or *darsi del tu;* that is, use the familiar "thou" form in Spanish, French, or Italian, as the case may be; and you find yourself lapsing back into *"Usted es muy amable"* instead of *"Tú eres muy amable"* ("You are very kind"); or, worse yet, if the lady of your dreams is a Russian, *"Ya Vas lyublyu"* instead of *"Ya tebya lyublyu"* where English "I love you" would present no implication that your affection was cooling.

When we come to the last of the age groups, we have another language problem. How to refer to senior citizens in a way that is at once respectful and not a sad reminder that the years are passing, particularly where they are concerned?

Suggestions are legion: "goldenager" is sticky sweet; "geriatric set" puts you into a mental wheelchair; "mature" implies that younger people aren't, and, anyhow, it's been preempted by purveyors of pornographic movies, books, and magazines; "venerable" is pretentious, and is a reminder of passing years, albeit a respectful one. Those seniors who are more sprightly come out with "nifty-fifty group," "sexy-sixty set," even "sensuous-seventy clique," but they are the exception rather than the rule. Europe's International Office for Social Tourism has come up with a name that is not bad, although it has political overtones: "the third age." But many senior citizens resent these terms, and choose to be viewed as persons. They deplore what they label "agism."

Senior citizens, their problems, and their potential power, are very much in the media and in the talk of politicians. A good deal has already been done for them, and far more has been promised. The trouble is that they don't have anything like the genius for political organization and clout that is so evident in the case of other groups, such as organized labor and the blacks. They are promised far more than they demand, but the promises are seldom kept by the politicians; they are skirted by the media. Here is one glaring example:

During the 1968 campaign, President Nixon (then candidate Nixon) appeared on a TV newsreel, which I saw and heard, before a large group of senior citizens in California. To them he said, "I pledge, if I am elected, to bring back full income-tax deductibility for medical expenses for people over sixty-five." This full deductibility was standard in income-tax regulations until the middle of the second Johnson administration, when without fanfare or notice the rules were changed, subjecting senior citizens to the same restrictions of 3 and 1 percent of income exclusion that prevail for others. It was perhaps thought that Medicare would take adequate care of senior citizens' medical expenses. But Medicare, and even Medicare Insurance, for which the senior citizen pays, have a deductible clause that keeps escalating upward; they also exclude any reimbursement of dental expenses, including dentures, and of ophthalmological expenditures, including eyeglasses. A senior citizen who is in reasonably good health and not in need of hospitalization or operations finds that these items, plus orthopedic appliances of all sorts, are up to him or her if they do not exceed 3 or 1 percent of income. This in turn means that senior citizens who are not classed as poor or destitute find themselves out of pocket far more today than they did in the bad old days before Medicare. After Nixon's 1968 election, the pledge was conveniently forgotten, and no one outside of me, apparently, offered a reminder. Letters written to various senators and congressmen of my acquaintance evoked evasive replies or went unanswered. Senator Harrison Williams of New Jersey stated that he had presented a bill making medical expenses of all sorts tax-deductible for everybody—a highly laudable step, but one that obviously had far less chance of passing than the restoration of full deductibility for the elderly. It, too, was forgotten. To my knowledge, no one else, the media included, offered any reminder of the campaign promise or objection to the new setup, which stands to this day. Most of the efforts of senior citizens, such as they are, are directed at bigger and better Social Security payments, which have more or less kept up with inflation, but still fail to solve many of the problems of the elderly.

Yet both media and politicians are forever sympathizing with the plight of senior citizens, some of whom apparently have no pensions, savings, or anything else beyond Social Security, and have been reported as eating dog food because practically all their Social Security money goes for rent and health care (No Medicaid? No savings of any kind?).

There is no dearth of other special groups that cannot be qualified by sex, age, or political or religious persuasion, yet constitute sizable minorities, which tend to organize on a nationwide basis: the handicapped, for whom special modifications are in the process of being introduced in buses and other means of transportation; the blind, for whom extensive Braille printings of books are made; the deaf-mutes, for whom TV sometimes inserts special boxes in sign language into regular programs. "Deaf Power and Pride" read the lapel button of demonstrators agitating for certain bills in their favor in Trenton, New Jersey. This group also reminds us that the term "deaf-mute" is no longer acceptable, presumably by reason of its "deaf-and-dumb" overtones. At any rate, many people who are physiologically only deaf have learned to speak.

In addition to these groups that base their affiliation on physical characteristics, there are many others united by similar tastes and preferences: nonalcoholics, nonsmokers, vegetarians, etc. The vegetarians recently proclaimed a "turkey liberation" week, advocating Thanksgiving dinners featuring grain-and-rice croquettes and "nonviolent" stuffing.

A few special classes do not fall into specific age groups and are rather loosely organized, but deserve special mention. They include hobos, many of whom are young adults, often college dropouts who can't stand the college atmosphere and the attitude of other students. One of these, on being interviewed, made an interesting distinction between hobos, bums, and tramps. The "hobo" travels whenever he can, and works at jobs only to be able to eat so he can travel more. "Tramps" are not interested in going places, while "bums" travel only when they are unwelcome where they happen to be. Hobos, he went on, never beg, while bums and tramps do. If this distinction holds water, the hobo would normally fall into a younger age group, the tramp and bum into an older category.

Then there are "witches," who describe themselves as "paganists," but not "Satan worshipers," have no blood rituals, orgies, or drug parties, believe in reincarnation and in an afterlife described as "Summerland." Witchcraft, they claim, is a religion, based on pagan beliefs that antedate Christianity. Magic is a gift from the gods, and "white magic" is used as Christians use prayer. When a witch enters a "coven," he or she takes a pagan or witch name, partly to protect his or her identity. In their "Sabbaths" they use a crystal ball, a censer, salt, water, bells, candles, and a knife called "Athemi." At coven meetings they are usually "skyclad" (naked), but at more public gatherings they wear red and black hooded robes. Their "Samhain," or Feast of the Dead, coincides with Halloween. While all age groups are included, paganism, in the words of a coven leader, "appeals mainly to younger people, because it offers them an ability to choose their life-style." They mean and do no harm, but often heal, and do good. They respect all life. It is not explained what purpose "Athemi," the knife, serves.

There is not too much of a political nature that can be charged against either hobos or witches, nor do they actively agitate for legislation in their favor. But they do appeal to the media, often in distorted fashion (witness the many films on Satanism). Also, there are "witch and warlock" shops that sell appropriate items. Hobos like Jack Kerouac have been known to cash in on their "profession" by writing best-sellers and giving lectures. A certain amount of favorable publicity, even if only personal, is always to be desired.

Groups such as the above are frankly representative of minority interests. They are to be kept distinct from other organizations that, rightly or wrongly, claim to act for the population as a whole. Typical of the latter are Ralph Nader's consumer groups (everyone is a consumer, from the person on welfare to the multimillionaire); or Common Cause, which claims to keep watch over legislation and politicians on behalf of the entire electorate; or the American Civil Liberties Union, which claims to protect the constitutional rights of all individuals and groups, regardless of their color or political philosophies. But these, too, are very much in the media.

One distressing phenomenon associated with the fragmentation of society into minority groups, many of which overlap, is brought out in an article entitled "The 'Rights' Explosion Splintering America?" (*U.S. News & World Report,* October 31, 1977). It is a well-known characteristic of our democratic structure that people have the right to organize into associations designed to protect their group interests and present their views, even with peaceful, if noisy, demonstrations. Many of these organized groups claim "rights" that lie quite outside and beyond the original Bill of Rights of the Constitution, but have more or less tenuous connections with various constitutional amendments passed since the founding of our nation. To the extent that a "right" is a "legal claim on an area of individual discretion," as stated by some dictionaries, the term tends to become increasingly confused, contradictory, and undefinable.

Do the rights of the individual or group include such things as picket lines and sit-in demonstrations, which infringe upon the rights of others to go about their legitimate business? Do minors have the "right" to make critical decisions for themselves, both in school and at home, including the right to abortion without parental consent? Do senior citizens have the "right" to keep on working past the age prescribed by mandatory-retirement programs? Do convicted prisoners have the "right" of access to a complete law library? Are there special "rights" for homosexuals, left-handed people, alcoholics, drug users, indigent women seeking free abortions, deserters denied military pensions?

The above groups include individuals who may also fall under such categories as black, Hispanic, American Indian, East Asian, or other racial or ethnic minorities, some of which demand as a right a "quota" system (call it "affirmative action" if you will) in employment or admission to institutions of higher learning that is quite at variance with our tradition of open competition based on merit, as was brought out in the Bakke case.

It is difficult for courts, even the Supreme Court, to decide on the constitutional aspects of all the "rights" that are advanced. It is even more difficult for the government bureaucrats to enforce the decisions. In one very recent case, the public library of Rudd, Iowa, a farming community of 429 inhabitants, was ordered to install a ramp making it possible for wheelchair users to avoid the three steps leading to the entrance. To the objection that there were no wheelchair cases among the town's residents, the HEW bureaucrats charged with enforcing the Congressional Rehabilitation Act of 1973 were obdurate: "You might some day have a wheel-chair user." Installing the ramp would entail considerable expense for a library whose total yearly expenditures are about $3,600. No matter. The law, once on the statute books, must be obeyed. Latest advice, however, is to the effect that HEW has relented, and granted permission to suspend the ramp until a wheelchair user actually appears in Rudd.

Many black organizations and writers present the thesis that present discrimination, even to the point of quota systems, is justified by past discrimination against the ancestors of the present generation.

A *Newark Star-Ledger* correspondent offers, perhaps with tongue in cheek, a somewhat complicated plan for the determination of quotas based on what he calls "PDF" ("past discrimination factor") "for each sexual, age, racial, ethnic, religious, nationally originated, and other genetically differentiated group," based on a comparison between each minority's population percentage and their percentage representation, and including consideration of all conditions existing in the United States since our country's birth. Then each of these numerical rankings would be multiplied by the total number of all the minority groups to which the candidate belongs, to arrive at his or her final ranking and order of precedence in jobs or admissions. This obvious *reductio ad absurdum* should take care, among other things, of our unemployment problem, since the number of existing bureaucrats would have to be at least doubled to work out the necessary calculations, even with the aid of IBM computers.

21 Science Speaks in Many Tongues

A sculptor, Robert Berks, has taken it upon himself to save our society from the fate of Babel, whose would-be builders forgot their common humanity and fell into a babble of tongues, with the results we all know. It is his contention that modern Babel affects not so much the lowly masses as the best and brightest minds, which have lost the power to communicate among themselves. The certified doctors of each discipline have devised invented vocabularies that are meaningless to their fellows in other fields. Being deeply versed in problems of energy, architecture, and sailing, Berks, with the help of his wife, whom he calls his "wordsmith," proposes to open up the mysteries of science, art, and human relations to the uninitiated, creating an Esperanto of science that will be accessible to all.

The concept is grandiose. Its fulfillment is doubtful. Dr. A. D. Kelly of Toronto, in the *CMA Journal* of October 5, 1974, graphically presents some of the difficulties. He starts with a list of scientifically used words to which he objects: "overview," "parameter," "continuum," "data retrieval," "crisis-oriented," "demotivational," "adhocratic," "logistical projection," "synergistical," "infrastructure," "to liaise," "software," "conceptualize," "thrust" are only a few. From his own field of medicine he selects "primary contact physician" (general practitioner), then links it up with educational-sociological parlance in "sexually active unmarried minors"; "exceptional children" (a euphemism for "underachievers," itself a euphemism for "retarded" or, Heaven save us, even "dull"); "socially deviant" and "sociopaths"; "psychotronics"; "biofeedback"; "bioenergetics"; "eidetic imagery"; and "drug subculture." All this he deplores. But how to change it?

Is there a weasely aspect to the vocabularies of science? The answer is yes. A large part of the unnecessary superstructure is motivated by a desire to achieve both professional prestige and financial profit. Do the media contribute their share to this phenomenon? Seldom in the sense that they initiate it; often in the sense that they pick it up, stress its sensational aspects, and broadcast it to their readers and viewers. Some of the evil seed falls on fertile ground, grips the popular imagination, and the terms get into the general language, often in erroneous or distorted form or meaning.

The field of modern science is so vast, its branches so numerous, that only a few can be discussed here. They are, however, fairly typical.

Medicine, in all its ramifications, is probably the science that most affects the general public. Here we have seen extraordinary advances coupled with dismal failures. Often the product that worked well in the test tube or the laboratory displayed its drawbacks (and they were often long-range) when it began to be used on human beings. The sulfa drugs, penicillin and other antibiotics, and cortisone are cases in point. True, many of them were modified on the basis of experience to the point of being made almost harmless. In the interim, how many lives were sacrificed on the altar of experimentation? Latest to come under discussion is Valium, a tranquilizer that has given rise to a half-billion-dollar-a-year industry. It seems that if it is overused there may be withdrawal symptoms that go all the way from tremors to epilepsylike convulsions, accompanied by a cold sweat. It has been described as the "opiate of the middle classes," but it has also been known to be used by junkies in substitution for stronger drugs.

In its political manifestations, medicine has led to the "socialized medicine" of Britain and other countries, and to our own Medicare and Medicaid, with their beneficial features, but also with their harmful ones, more and more of which come to the surface every day. Medicare costs, needless operations, hospitalizations, and surgery, along with malpractice insurance rates, have climbed astronomically.

Economic motivation abundantly explains the publicitarian aspects of the propaganda created by certain medical fields, especially the drug manufacturers. What it fails to explain, save indirectly, is the morbid fascination of the new media, radio and especially TV, with disease and self-styled disease prevention, with surgery and operations, with physicians and their problems, both real and imaginary. "Young Doctor Kildare" has had time to become "Old," even "Decrepit," Dr. Kildare. "Marcus Welby," "General Hospital," "M.A.S.H.," dozens of programs, including even the medical-surgical angle on "The Rookies," have familiarized us with disease and its cure, bringing both perennially into the focus of our consciousness. News items such as the breast cancer operations of Betty Ford and Happy Rockefeller (not fiction, but reality) have been used as themes for the early discovery and treatment of such diseases, with the possibility of unnecessary surgery and harmful radiation from the excess of X-ray examinations. Add to this the constant description of possible symptoms of innumerable diseases presented in commercials by drug companies; the claims, often retracted at the behest of federal watchdogs, made for some of the products ("Listerine kills germs"; so does alcohol; swish with Scotch?); the often disgusting commercial discussions of deodorants, feminine hygiene, stomach acidity, "Preparation Itch," and many minor ailments—and you have enough to turn your stomach and make you turn off your set. But over and above this, there is the danger of turning us into a nation of hypochondriacs, living in constant fear of hundreds of obscure yet well-publicized ailments, running to our doctor or clinic for reassurance. Actually, this is the least of the evils, because the doctor is the only one who can properly interpret the symptoms we have, or think we have on the basis of what we hear in commercials. Unfortunately, not all doctors give us an honest evaluation, though the great majority of them do. There is a special term, "Ping-Ponging," which is Medicare-Medicaid parlance for the practice of referring the patient to a battery of specialists, each of whom collects from the patient or, more often, from the taxpayers.

Someone has gone to the trouble of making a list of the ten most common scare-words in the field of medicine and disease prevention: "aerosol," "cholesterol," "cyclamates," "carcinogen," "allergy," "hypertension," "pollutant," "radiation," "zone," "counseling" (the last for psychiatric ailments). Three others may be added from the area of food adulterants: "additive," "coloring," "nitrite."

How many unnecessary or useless tests and operations are due to the scare propaganda carried on by the drug manufacturers, a small part of the medical profession, and the media? These are figures that will never be revealed, for who is to judge? Also, they must be set off against the very real advantage of causing people to go in for a medical checkup, which may reveal a very real condition of which the patient had no suspicion, but which comes to the surface in the course of the examination meant to allay his fears of something else.

One physician has had the courage to state that in addition to the unnecessary practices, there are also those which are known in advance to be perfectly useless by reason of the advanced age and general deterioration of the patient. But here we enter the highly controversial field of euthanasia.

One myth merits exploding. We are often told that life expectancy, which was thirty or thereabouts in antiquity and the

Middle Ages, has been advanced to seventy or beyond by the progress of medical science. This is in part true, in part distorted. The average life expectancy has been prolonged largely by the fact that the high death rate of women in childbirth and of infants in their first year has been drastically cut down. Many forms of pestilence have been conquered, though others have risen to take their place. Despite the fearsome destructiveness of modern warfare, more people died by violence in the past than they do in the present, in proportion to the existing population. A survey of the known life span of important people in antiquity and the Middle Ages, who had obviously surmounted the childbirth and first-year hurdles, indicates that barring those hurdles, plus death by violence, the life span has not appreciably increased. The Bible's "threescore and ten" would seem to point to the same conclusion. Which does not mean that we should not be thankful for what has been achieved.

There are not too many terms in the medical field that lend themselves to humorous treatment, outside of spoofs like Sonny and Cher's "Heartbreak of Psoriasis" and the use of "Dermatitis" as a character in a pseudo historical sketch. One is "paramedics" for people who are not quite doctors, though they function more or less as such; which leads one wit to suggest "parapatients" for people who only think they're sick. Another is "triage," not yet admitted to some dictionaries, but said to have arisen during World War II from a widespread medical practice of separating the wounded into three groups: those who would get well without treatment, those who would die no matter what, and those who might be saved if given care. Only the wounded in the last category were given treatment—a seemingly heartless procedure, but one made necessary by the scarcity of doctors and medical supplies. The word has recently been applied to problems of food scarcity in an overpopulated world, and the question of how the relatively few nations endowed with agricultural surpluses should treat the pleas of overcrowded countries stricken by drought and other disasters. Euthanasia for nations, as well as for individuals?

The medical profession on occasion turns linguistically creative in the popular as well as the scientific field. "Cope" not followed by "with" is termed "informal" in most of our dictionaries, and is rejected by a majority of *American Heritage*'s experts. Yet a prominent medical magazine *(MD)* features in its advertising the new term "copelessness," used more or less as a synonym for depression.

In the "Medi-" family, Australia has recently added "Medipet," insurance for veterinary fees; but this is run by a private insurance company, not by the government. There is also "Medifraud," devised by an investigator into the many abuses of both Medicare and Medicaid. Then there is "angel dust," an animal tranquilizer ("phenocyclide" is its official name), which is occasionally used as a drug for human beings. It produces hallucinations, and can even kill. There is the controversy about giving a more precise and scientific name to "Legionnaires' Disease," which the American Legion has gone on record as opposing. They seem to be rather proud of it.

Of general interest is a recently published list of uncommon phobias, which are the immediate concern of psychologists and psychiatrists. Beginning with "claustrophobia" (fear of closed spaces), we go on to "agoraphobia" (fear of open spaces), and "acrophobia" (fear of heights). Closely allied are "kremnophobia" (fear of steep places; from Greek *kremnos*, "crag, steep cliff"); "kenophobia" (fear of empty spaces; Greek *kenos*, "empty"); and "bathophobia" (not fear of baths, but fear of depths; Greek *bathys*, "deep").

"Anthropophobia" (Greek *anthropos*, "man, mankind") is fear of human society. But there is also "androphobia" (Greek *aner*, root *andr-*, "man, male"), fear of man as a male, which is paralleled by "gynophobia" (*gyne*, "woman"), fear of women as a sex. Both sexes may suffer in common from "gamophobia" (*gamos,* "wedding"), fear of marriage. Psychologically related, perhaps, is "haptephobia" (*hapto,* "to fasten on to something or someone"), fear of being touched. "Demophobia" (*demos,* "people") is fear of crowds. "Dromophobia" (*dromos,* "road"; appearing also in "hippodrome," which is a horse-race course) is fear of crossing streets and roads.

On the purely mythological side is "Friggaphobia," fear of Fridays. Frigga was the Norse goddess, wife of Odin, after whom Friday was named, and she supplies the only Teutonic element in what is otherwise pure Greek. There is a "mythophobia" (Greek *mythos,* "fable, myth"), but it is used for fear of telling or being told lies.

"Sitophobia" (*sitos,* "food") is fear of eating, and "hypnophobia" (*hypnos,* "sleep") is fear of falling asleep. "Hedonophobia" is fear of pleasure *(hedone),* and "bibliophobia" (*biblos,* "book") is the fear of books that some teenagers and others suffer from. Some phobias are more psychological than real. "Autophobia" (*autos,* "self") is not fear of autos ("automobile," the full form, is a Greek-Latin hybrid, "self-movable"), but of oneself. "Eremophobia" (*eremos,* "solitary, lonesome") is fear of lonesomeness; "hypengyophobia" (*hypengyos,* "responsible") is fear of responsibility. "Rhabdophobia" (*rhabdos* was a wand, twig, or rod, and the last was often used for chastisement) is fear of being bested or defeated; while "atephobia" (*ate,* "ruin") is fear of being ruined.

Two somewhat deplorable phobias are "neophobia" (*neos,* "new"), which is fear of innovations, and for which "ideophobia" (fear of new ideas) can be a suitable substitute; and "xenophobia" (*xenos,* "stranger, foreigner"), fear of strangers or foreigners, which often reaches the point of hatred.

Then there are some really bad phobias, which start with "algophobia", fear of pain *(algos);* "toxicophobia," fear of poison (*toxon* is a bow, but it often shot poisoned arrows); and "ophidophobia" (*ophis,* "snake"), fear of snakes. They go all the way on to "thanatophobia" (*thanatos,* "death"), fear of death, and "taphetophobia" (*taphos,* "burial"), fear of being buried alive.

And remember, this is only a partial list. With the aid of a Greek dictionary, and a bit of knowledge of Greek you can make up your own pet phobia. If it hasn't already been coined, I have coined one for myself: "chionodromophobia" (*chion,* "snow") for my pet aversion to driving on snow and ice.

One distressing fact about medicine and the medical profession is the declining confidence that the population at large reposes in them, which goes *pari passu* (right along) with the decline in confidence in government and governmental institutions. There is more than a possibility of a direct link between the two phenomena, as government tends more and more to take over medical practice. A recent Harris poll indicates that confidence in the medical profession declined from 73 to 43 percent between 1966 and 1977. During the same period, confidence in the executive branch of government slipped from 41 to 23 percent; in Congress, from 42 to 17 percent; so the medical profession is still far ahead of government in the people's trust.

Medicare-Medicaid straddles both camps. But there are additional factors, not the least of which are the conflicting expert opinions of the medical profession itself with regard to certain measures that have won government approval, such as the ban on saccharin, or the swine flu immunization shots. Some people wonder why, if the government feels it is necessary to ban saccharin, it doesn't also feel the necessity of banning alcohol, at least in concentrated forms, and cigarettes, for the harmful effects of which the medical evidence is much stronger (there are, of course, economic and tax revenue factors involved). Laetrile is another case in point. One of the harmful manifestations of this spirit of distrust is that children are not being immunized as they should be against such common diseases as polio, measles, and mumps.

The aura of infallibility that both government and medical science have built around themselves is too often dispelled by tragic errors. Perhaps both should assume a greater attitude of humility, and acknowledge that they, too, can make mistakes.

The old, traditional branches of science, physics, chemistry, biology, while they have all made giant advances in recent times, with vast vocabulary expansion, do not lend themselves to weaselism, since they deal with material things and processes that are fully measurable. Furthermore, their basic vocabularies, fixed in the nineteenth and early twentieth centuries, are stable, in the sense that they can be built upon without excessive flights of the imagination.

This is not altogether true of the most recent additions to the vast field of science and technology: space, atomic science, computer science. These enjoy highly spectacular features that appeal to the media, which report them and attempt to describe them and make them intelligible to the nonspecialist. To the extent that they are linked to problems of defense, they enter the political arena, with propaganda for and against higher appropriations. The profit motive is also inherent in the manufacturers of equipment connected with them, and this is to some extent in evidence in the form both of advertising and of slanted presentations in the media.

It would be idle in this book to try to go into these matters in depth, but a few linguistic creations may be of interest. One spoofer who describes the adventures of an imaginary professor who travels all over the world on research missions offers two words economical of space and time: "spacicle" for space vehicle, and "astricle" for astronautical. A newspaper writer, having made the acute observation that Soviet space vehicles normally come down on land, not in the water, coins "thumpdown" on the analogy of our "splashdown." Astronauts and cosmonauts give rise to "Ufonauts" for people who believe in unidentified flying objects. In more conventional air flying, the Concorde controversy has given rise to the term "retrofit," which is the placing of noise-abating materials in overnoisy planes.

Atomic studies have brought to light one more hypothetically indivisible unit of matter, beyond the proton and the neutron, and this has been labeled the "quark," hypothesized as the ultimate building block of "hadrons," the whole class of heavy particles (the term is said to have been appropriated from a whimsical line in James Joyce). This occurred as far back as 1962, but now certain hypothetical qualities have been attributed to quarks to explain observed phenomena. Quarks are now said to come in three "colors" and four "flavors" (more may be added later). Also, eight varieties of "gluons" are needed to explain the forces that bind the quarks together into hadrons. Lastly, one more property has been added, "charm," an arbitrary term having to do with whether the quark belongs to matter or antimatter. If all this strikes the nonphysicist as somewhat confusing, well, it is.

In the more conventional field of physics, the energy crisis has brought into existence what might be described as "Solarspeak," an embryonic language connected with the equally embryonic use of solar energy. Here we have such dubious terms as "energy management systems" (ordinary drapes and awnings to you); "passive solar collectors" (just plain windows that let the sun's rays into a room); "valves of natural phenomena" (a collective term for doors and windows).

"Antisound," the coinage of Professor J. E. Ffoncs-Williams, an engineering scientist, goes to join "antimatter." He theorizes that since sound travels through the air in waves of pressure that have tops and troughs, like ocean waves, an annoying sound could be wiped out by generating another sound of exactly the same wavelength and waveheight, but whose tops would coincide with the troughs of the other sound, and vice versa. The result would be utter silence, as the two waves would cancel each other out.

The theory has yet to be put to a complete scientific test, but its possibilities might be of interest to sponsors of the Concorde airplane and to opponents of traffic and other constant sources of noise.

Computer terminology is in a different class, as the computer becomes more and more a participant in our daily lives. We have long been familiar with the bank computer, which at one fell swoop registers your deposit or withdrawal and the current state of your account. Modest, but latest addition to the field is the supermarket "scanner" that permits the checker to pass most items over it and have them recorded, with their description and price, on your receipt; one of the biggest time- and labor-savers of recent times.

Philip J. Freedenberg of the Riverside Research Institute in New York City has been kind enough to supply me with some choice bits of computer language and slang. Some of these are acronyms: "DAC" for "digital-to-analog computer"; "MUX" for "multiplexer"; "LED" for "light emitting diode." Others are abbreviated or telescoped forms: "PUFFS" for "picofarads"; "MEGS" for "megohms"; "SYNC" or "SYNC UP" for "synchronize." Facetiously slangy are "GEZINTA" and "GEZOUTA" ("goes into" and "goes out of," for "input" and "output"; nothing for "throughput"? May I suggest "GEZTHROUGH"?); "SUB" for "subcontractor"; "KLUGE" for unwieldy machine; "FUDGE" for unorthodox programming trick that achieves the desired results; "HONCHO" for chief engineer; "YEA BY YEA" for hand-gestured way of conveying dimensions. "REDEYE" in Computerese is not cheap whiskey, but a west-to-east transcontinental flight arriving at dawn; a "BIMB" is a rental car.

The computer language makes abundant use of terms from the "new mathematics," thus establishing a link with the "new education." A "BIT" is a "binit" or binary unit, and eight bits make a "BYTE"; but four bits are a "HEX." A "GLITCH" is a local anomaly in a set of data.

A list of prefixes worth memorizing, if you are interested, is the following: "MEGA-"—1,000,000; "MILLI-"—.001; "MICRO-" —.000001; "NANO-"—.000000001; "PICO-"—.000000000001. "MINI-," on the other hand, simply means minicomputer.

Two additional terms have seeped into the language of ham radio operators and CB artists: "SNAKE ON THE LOOSE"— "there are technical difficulties while on the air"; "GALLON" —kilowatt.

Distantly related to Computerese is a commercial term devised by MCA: "VIDISK"—movies on minifilms (not tapes) designed for home viewing of complete movies, and retailing at $15 (but the player unit is around $500).

The language of psychology, like the social sciences in general, is interspersed through both commercial advertising and political propaganda. It is nothing if not controversial, since it deals with the functioning of the human (or even the animal) mind, which is not yet subject to precise measurements or generalizations of the physical science type. Extreme views and attitudes in the field have given rise to equally extreme reactions. Some decry the social sciences in general and the various branches of psychology, psychiatry, and psychoanalysis in particular. Others limit themselves to mild ridicule, like the journalist who described "psychoceramics" as the study of cracked pots. Then there was the one who, describing U.S. concern with the study of Puerto Ricans on the mainland and its link with the problems of the high incidence of poverty, unemployment, underemployment, as well as civil rights, went on to remark that the study of such so-called problem groups as Puerto Ricans amounts to an industry within the social sciences; a charge of weaselism that may have some basis.

The latest development in the field is "psychohistory," which combines the insights of psychology and psychoanalysis with the data of history. This can be carried on for both dead and living subjects. It is reported that President Carter will soon be the subject of a full-scale psychobiography. In this and similar connections, the American Psychiatric Association feels that serious ethical and scholarly questions remain unsolved. There is in particular the risk of invasion of privacy. "Psychoprofiles" of the living have on occasion been compiled by intelligence agencies "in the service of the national interest" (the Ellsberg break-in is a case in point, and we know what storms that aroused). In the case of living subjects, should the psychobiography be done only with the subject's express permission? Sigmund Freud did a psychobiography of sorts of Leonardo da Vinci, discussing in particular the subject's illegitimate birth, his mother's excessive tenderness, leading to sexual repression that affected his later life. Leonardo was not, of course, available for comment. But when Nixon's "emotional tragedy" is discussed in a book that claims that the subject was haunted by a sense of guilt for the death of his brothers, which in turn led both to his ambition and his self-inflicted isolation, we may yet hear from the subject.

The theory that President Carter is "thrice born," with a second birth at the time of his father's death in 1953, and a third with his conversion experience of the middle 1960s, also lends itself to comment and criticism by the living subject. At any rate, "psychohistory," "psychobiography," "psychoprofile" (the last said to be a regular professional practice with the CIA) seem to have entered the language to stay. Needless to say, books and articles done in this vein lend themselves to commercial advertising, political use, and abundant media discussion, slanted or otherwise.

Somewhat along the same line is the theory advanced by Professor Roger E. Bennett of Ohio State University that split-second facial expressions, known as "micromomentaries," occur at the precise moment a person is telling a lie, even in the case of psychopathic liars who are able to beat polygraph tests. Having once been a journalist, he hopes that his discovery will be a reporter's tool that will enable press interviewers to tell when their hostile subjects are lying. Videotapes, he claims, show that the human subconscious produces bizarre expressions around the face, characterized by rapid eye movements, when a falsehood is uttered. The micromomentaries take place at one-sixtieth of a second, while normal blinking takes one-fifth of a second.

The field of linguistics, with which I am directly acquainted, has long been outstanding for its overproductivity in the matter of terminology, and there is no use belaboring a point I have already made elsewhere.

It may be of interest, however, to cull from a long list of linguistic works produced by the University Linguistic Club of the University of Indiana a few choice titles illustrative of both the terminology and the mental processes involved: "On the Linguistic Status of the Performative-Contrastive Distinction"; "Extrinsic Ordering Lives"; "Conjunction Reduction, Gapping, Hacking, and the Preservation of Surface Structure"; " 'Gut Feelings' in Generative Grammar"; "Global Constraints on Quantifiers and Adverbs"; "Phylogenetic Reflections of Ontogenic Processes"; "Hedged Performatives"; "The Precyclic Nature of Predicate Raising"; "Can the 'Elsewhere Condition' Get Anywhere?"; "Adverbs and Opacity"; "On Identifying the Remains of Deceased Clauses"; "If Speakers Can't Count Syllables, What Can They Do?"; "Verbs of Bitching."

I know not how others may feel, but for myself, I like the last two titles best.

22 Education's Forked Tongue

The story of education in America is a strange one. Deemed so unimportant at the time of the founding of the Republic that it was not even mentioned in the original Constitution, and so left by implication to the discretion of the states and the people, it has grown into a Behemoth that makes it mandatory for all children to be schooled through eight elementary grades, and often through four additional high-school years. By dint of propaganda exercised partly through the sympathetic media, partly through political channels, it has succeeded in firmly implanting into the popular mind two more axioms that are not at all necessarily true: first, that a college education is highly desirable, not for reasons of culture, but because it is the gateway to better and higher-paying jobs; second, applicable in some communities, that this college education at the expense of the taxpayers should be at the disposal of all, regardless of intellectual qualifications, interest in what colleges have to offer, or prior preparation.

How have these peculiar states of mind been achieved? It is a well-known fact that in other civilized lands, both democratic and totalitarian, six to eight years of elementary education are normally available to all, and that such education is free, compulsory, and universal, as it is with us. Beyond that, educational advancement is determined by one of two factors: first, superior intellectual attainment by the individual, as determined by previous preparation and standardized tests; or, second, by family wealth, or, in totalitarian countries, by family political connections. This does not exclude trade schools, where training in manual occupations may be acquired. A reasonable balance seems to be indicated by statistics for such countries as Great Britain and the Soviet Union, where roughly 25 percent of elementary-school graduates go on to the equivalents of our high schools, and roughly 25 percent of high-school graduates go on to the equivalents of our colleges and universities. This gives the nation a potential supply of, very roughly, 75 percent manual workers of all kinds, many of whom may turn out to be highly skilled in their calling, with high wage scales and other benefits; 20 percent white-collar workers; and 5 percent professionals (doctors, lawyers, engineers, researchers, professors, clergymen), plus higher executives in business, industry, and government.

By reason of the first axiom described above, American society is burdened with a perennial oversupply of professionals and executives (particularly lawyers, professors, clergymen, and bureaucrats); an occasional oversupply of white-collar workers; and an occasional over- or undersupply of manual workers. The last two depend on business conditions and the state of the economy.

There has recently been some questioning of the inalienable "right" of all people who want it to a college education at public expense, along with suggestions for reform. One such suggestion, voiced by a committee headed by New Jersey State Education Commissioner Fred G. Burke, has some appealing features, including the abolition of some legal constraints prohibiting adolescents from working, such as excessively stringent child-labor laws and minimum-wage restrictions. In addition, the commission recommends an "entitlement program," guaranteeing every person in the state fifteen years of free education, from kindergarten to sophomore year in college; such entitlement would continue through each person's lifetime, so that one could interrupt his or her studies, go to work, and resume the educational pursuits at any time that was convenient.

Viewing the situation from another angle, the status of the educator in the United States has been subjected to drastic fluctuations in the course of the last hundred years. A dichotomy between schoolteachers and university professors was established about a century ago, with the former charged with teaching functions in elementary and high schools, the second etherialized into an intellectual élite mainly concerned with "research." The same is to some extent true of other countries, but with one important difference. The line of demarcation elsewhere is drawn between the university and secondary educational institutions, whether these are labeled *Gymnasium, lycée,* or by some other name. In the United States, there is a four-year something that intervenes between elementary and high school on the one hand, the university as a fully graduate school on the other. That something is the undergraduate college, which partakes of the characteristics of both, at least so far as faculties are concerned.

There are in existence far more undergraduate colleges than there are true universities. But the universities worthy of the name (Harvard, Yale, Columbia, Princeton, to name a few) invariably carry undergraduate departments that function as colleges. Ambitious, expansion-minded college administrators, on the other hand, seize every possible opportunity to put in a few graduate departments, and relabel themselves universities. In most other countries, universities function almost totally as research institutions, generally with endowed chairs for each topic or field. The various *Gymnasia* and *lycées,* on the other hand, function almost exclusively as teaching-and-learning institutions. Their work naturally involves a certain amount of research, which need not be original, but can be restricted to compilation and interpretation of the original work of others. This means that the work of such foreign institutions can at the most be compared, on the American plane, with graduate work on the M.A., but not the Ph.D., level.

The confusion in our colleges and their faculties is caused by the fact that while most of the actual work of the staff lies in the field of imparting knowledge to the students (for which teaching ability is required), the pressure exerted by the administrations is for the instructing staff to prove that they are, first and foremost, researchers, because this justifies the institution's claim to be a "university." Here the famous slogan "publish or perish" comes into play. If you don't "produce," in the form of learned or pseudo-learned (that is, "scholarly") books, articles, and reviews, you don't advance and may be fired, no matter how effective and brilliant a classroom teacher you are. The qualities that go into a good classroom teacher and those that go into a good research scholar are occasionally, but not too often, to be found in the same person. More often the good classroom teacher is an outgoing communicator with a dynamic, inspiring personality, who prefers working with students to poring over musty volumes; while the researcher is often a timid, withdrawn person, a poor speaker, even if he is a brilliant writer and attains logical conclusions. To demand a full measure of both sets of qualities of the same individual is more often than not an exercise in futility. Yet the expediency of expansion demands that the colleges vie in scholarly output with the universities.

At the lower end of the academic scale are the elementary and high-school teachers, who are under no compulsion to prove themselves scholars, but must stand or fall on their teaching ability (plus, of course, a reasonable knowledge of the subject they teach). This area, in the elementary schools, has traditionally functioned with a majority of women, though the modern tendency is toward sexual equality, in numbers as well as in treatment. In the past, women were regarded as being more docile than men, as requiring less in the way of salaries and benefits, and as being more prone to follow rules set down by school boards, even where unreasonable.

This, in former years, led to a low regard for the teaching profession among administrators, politicians, even parents. The woman teacher was a "schoolmarm." The man teacher was someone who took to teaching because he couldn't make his way in the business world. Even the scholarly university professor was lampooned as an impractical fuddy-duddy (only occasionally, as in the Sherlock Holmes stories, was he portrayed as a mastermind of evil: Professors Moriarty and Moran).

For more years than I care to remember, the teacher, at all levels, was underpaid, overworked, imposed upon. Finally, there were two reactions that came almost simultaneously, mainly by reason of manpower shortages brought about by World War II and the subsequent business and industrial expansion. Likely candidates began to stay away in droves from taking up teaching as a career; while teachers, having before them the constant example of the labor unions, began to unionize in earnest instead of relying upon purely professional and scholarly associations that had no concern with material and economic problems.

But unionization carried with it its own peculiar abuses: excessive demands, picket lines, strikes. It is slightly disingenuous for teachers who go on strike and close the schools to claim that they are acting in the interests of the children who are deprived of their instruction. The fact that such a claim is often made is a relic of the old mentality that regarded teachers as dedicated, selfless persons whose main, not to say only, concern was with the progress of their pupils. Yet teacher unions are here to stay, and the problem, as with all unions, is how to reconcile their justified or unjustified demands with the general welfare of the community which they serve, but of which they are also an integral part.

Education has, of course, a specialized vocabulary; in fact, many specialized vocabularies, ranging all the way from the "pedaguese" of elementary instruction to the rarefied tongue of the scholars. Do these many tongues lend themselves to weasely ends? Are they often designed to confuse and bamboozle not only the layman, the parents, the general public, but even the politician who makes himself the spokesman for educational demands, and the demanders themselves, acting in a sort of self-induced hypnosis? The answer has to be in the affirmative. Do the media make themselves the mouthpieces of the educational lingo and the educational point of view? Yes, with qualifications. While they consciously or unconsciously spread the educational propaganda, they are also foremost in satirizing the excesses of the language of education.

Complaints fall under two major headings: on the one hand, both those who are taught and those who teach not only can't read or write, but can't even speak correctly. Says one correspondent, "Has the letter *T* dropped out of the alphabet? Listen to 'I wanna do this,' 'I'm gonna do that,' 'twenny,' 'plenny,' 'innerested.'" A picketing teacher in Chicago told a TV reporter, "I'm livin' on da near nort side now." Another teacher asked, "Do ya like it dere?"; while a third, just back from Ireland, on being asked "Where in Ireland did you go?," replied "Edinburgh."

At the more literate end of the spectrum, Robert J. Braun, reviewing Brian Hall's *The Development of Consciousness*, reports the following examples of linguistic creativity, unsanctioned by existing dictionaries: "consciousization," "ecority," "minessence."

A Rutgers professor of English thunders out against "Doublespeak," a language used by his fellow academicians, as well as by politicians, to deceive, mislead, or cover up. Some of his examples: "inner city" for "slum"; a college president asking for a list of employees to be "retrenched" ("fired"); "encore tele-

casts" for "TV reruns." Samples from other sources: "underachiever" for "poor student"; which leads a wit to coin a term
for its opposite, a teacher who is an "overexpecter"; an educator's definition of education's purpose as "skilling" (imparting
skills). James Kilpatrick, reporting on a three-day "workshop"
conducted by some fifty Ph.D.s, sponsored in Washington, D.C.,
by the National Institute of Education, samples some of the
contents of the report that emerged: "career interest invento-
ries," "the generic he" (which must be stricken from the English language because it is sexist); "lodging quarters cleaners"
and "waiter's assistants" for chambermaids and busboys. But
the final summary also contained: "concensus," "vetinarians,"
"sexually bivolent," "in the interum," "vigilent." Cost to the
taxpayers: $67,373.

The ultimate in educational-political weaselism is perhaps
best illustrated by the tactics employed in securing passage of
a state income tax in New Jersey to comply with a weasely
requirement of a "thorough and efficient education" (not otherwise defined), imposed by the state constitution and enforced
by a mandate of the state supreme court, closing all New Jersey
public schools until it was complied with by the recalcitrant
state legislature, which had heard from its constituents and
knew that it was risking political suicide to pass the tax. The
intervening discussion brought forth such gems as "T and E is
'do-able' " (just as clear as before); "funding" T and E education
(a euphemism for finding the money for it; but "funding"
smacks of funds and foundations, and some taxpayers are misled
into thinking that the money will come from such institutions
rather than from their own pockets). There was also a proposal
to "decentralize" public education, which turned out to mean
just the opposite, with policies set by the state education authorities rather than by local school boards, with a view to
establishing "goals and standards" applicable to all public
schools in the state. There was talk of "minimum performance
standards" and "maximum citizen involvement," "competency

to be internalized by the learner," "macrochange strategics that may be used in support of a humanistic educational organization," much loose talk about attitudes, values, feelings, openness of communication, diagnosing problems, "outcome goals" and "process goals," "meaningful relationship" to the present or future needs and/or interests of students, "structured competition" among students. Very little was said about teaching the students to read, write acceptable English, perform elementary arithmetical operations. All this was said to add up to "quality education," an expression that to me is reminiscent of "quality folks" and has a slightly aristocratic tinge (but this is purely a personal reaction, and may be discounted as such).

"Modelog," further described as a "Catalog of Comprehensive Educational Planning Component Models," is a 265-page book issued by the New Jersey State Department of Education, and designed to assist school boards in their planning. It "introduces the multi-dimensional efforts involved in conducting a full program evaluation. The focus is paroramic [sic] rather than microscopic." There are "indicators of sought-after outcomes," "organizational decision-making strategics," "discrepancy evaluation," "critical incidents," "defensible goals." There are also "negative behavior," "creativity," "preparing for world change," but again, not too much about learning to read, write, and cipher.

As one might expect, this philosophy is reflected in a good many courses and textbooks. One class of the latter is described as "educating with love," or the "touchy-feely" theory of education, where everyone loves and helps everyone else, and the teacher is called by his or her first name, or, better yet, a nickname. An excellent system if it can be made to work. At the other end of educational philosophy we find "planned paddlehood," for corporal punishment of recalcitrant and troublemaking students, British style.

Looking at other sections of the country, columnist Mike Royko supplies a few rare flowers culled from a bureaucratic memo issued to the Chicago school system by its superintendent: "Goals: to promote and reinforce the concept that the school facility is a functional extension of the instructional program . . . All key responsibilities and performance objectives are explicit methods and techniques of adopted policy implementation . . . a high degree of flexibility in order to reflect possible shifts in priorities, reassessment of feasibility factors, or a change in legal requirements."

On the other hand, there are some seemingly worthwhile educational experiments going on, such as the one in Toppenish, Washington, where the children are taught three languages and cultures at once: English, Spanish (there are many Mexicans in the area), and Yakima, the tongue of the local Indians. Learning a concept in a second or third language tends to reinforce that concept in the first language, and to create a world awareness, according to the innovators, a theory that impresses me as sound on the basis of observation and personal experience. Even more significant is the Soviet-American teacher exchange program sponsored by the American Field Service. Six Soviet high-school teachers and principals came recently to American high schools for a month of teaching Russian classes. The experiment, by all accounts, met with signal success from the standpoint of both Soviet teachers and American pupils. The latter got a truly broadening insight into the ways and customs of the vast Soviet world, while the former spoke glowingly of what they had learned about our life-style and system of education. It is to be hoped that both countries will profit from their experiences.

Unfortunately, not all visiting teachers from other countries are as favorably impressed by our school system. A group of ten teachers from as many African countries, ranging from Cameroon and Zaire to Tanzania and South Africa, found that while our school buildings were impressive, our classes small in comparison to theirs (classes of fifty are common in most African countries), and our books and scientific equipment plentiful and

up-to-date, American high-school students were sloppy in dress
and manners, deficient in discipline and in their attitude toward
homework and respect for their teachers, elders, and environment. For what concerns school administration, they unani-
mously deplored our lack of uniform standards in grading and
promoting. A ministry of education official from Cameroon inquired how we could evaluate student progress when the A of
one school was the equivalent of the C of another. "No uniform
testing, no national examinations to get a diploma!" was her
main complaint.

Shifting the spotlight from lower to higher education, we find
college education defined by a humorist as "the great training
robbery"; a course titled "Stone Age Survival" misinterpreted,
perhaps willfully, as having to do with "beating stones together," with the result that it was turned from straight archae-
ology into constructing shelters, reproducing stone tools, and
preparing animal skins.

"Open admission" to college to anyone holding a high-
school diploma, no matter how achieved, has led to the institution of numerous remedial courses, sometimes rebaptized
"developmental" to soften the impact. Here the students are
given instruction, with college credit, in the things they
should have learned in elementary and high school, notably
how to read, write, add, and subtract. At Berkeley, nearly half
the new entrants were found to need such instruction. Most
popular of the remedial courses was "Bonehead English," designed to teach the students how to express their thoughts
clearly on paper. But many refuse to feel inferior, and insist
on "doing their own thing," even rewriting the rules of grammar to suit themselves. George Orwell once said that "if people cannot write well, they cannot think well; and if they cannot think well, others will do their thinking for them." More
recently, August Heckscher, in the *Christian Science Monitor*
of March 19, 1976, declared: "That a large number of edu-

cated Americans are incapable of writing clearly is one of the notorious scandals of our national life." He went on to quote the editor of the *Yale Alumni Magazine* to the effect that letters received from his readers "are simply too fuzzy to be understood, and most are strewn with errors of grammar, syntax, usage, and spelling." In the same issue of the *Yale Alumni Magazine* Professor Bartlett Giamatti, director of the Division of the Humanities, described the so-called free speech movement of 1964, devised not only to "free speech from middle-class constraints, but also from the shackles of syntax, the racism of grammar, the elitism of style." This Giamatti summarizes as "a blow struck on behalf of feeling against intellect—on behalf of the mass against individualism." The consequences? A generation given over to essential sentimentality, replacing words with the inanities of drugs and loud music, and in the process losing the art of writing. Both writers express their hope in a coming reaction among the youth.

What of the popular attitude toward scholars and professors? Has it changed from the prewar days when the professor was viewed as a pompous, impractical nincompoop? Not too much, as witnessed by an example on the Johnny Carson program. Giving a list of collective nouns, profession by profession, to parallel "a pride of lions" and "a covey of partridges" in the animal world, Johnny came out with "a pomposity of professors."

It is not too often that professional (or professorial) features are brought directly to the attention of individuals to whom they are imputed. But a stranger on the phone, commenting about an article I had written, charged me also with having an "academic pronunciation." (Of course, he may have read my background at the end of the article.) Then he went on to prove it to me on the basis of my "suprasegmental phonemes." The two that stuck in my mind were: prolongation of the stressed syllables, and raising the pitch at the end of the sentence. In other words, I am not immune.

Perhaps because of its pomposity, the scholarly world often lends itself to hoaxes and flimflams. One case recently reported was that of three Southern California medical educators who hired a professional actor, dressed him up with a fictitious *curriculum vitae,* and presented him to lecture to groups of psychiatrists, psychologists, and social workers on the topic of "Mathematical Game Theory as Applied to Physical Education." The self-styled Dr. Myron Fox of Albert Einstein University lectured to the fifty-five educators, using academic jargon and double-talk, and making irrelevant, conflicting, and meaningless statements, both in his lectures and in the following question-and-answer periods. The comments of the audience? "Excellent presentation"; "Has warm manner"; "Lively examples"; "Extremely articulate." There was a single note of doubt: "Too intellectual." Not one of the audience saw through the phony, and all were convinced they had learned something.

Milder and more obvious flimflams, exemplifying what one critic has called "leximegalomania," include a letter sent out to its membership by the Yale Alumni Fund at the end of 1975, sporting such words as "gardyloo," "amphoric," "borborygm," "rectalgia," "epigamic," "frocteur" (one who gets kicks from rubbing against people in crowds), "nothosomia" (calling someone a bastard), "alpha betterments" (bureaucracy), "yauld," "Kneippism," "pagophagia." Some of these terms are in the dictionary. The writers, seemingly unsure of their own creation, supplied a glossary at the end of the letter.

There is some slight consolation for the low state of our educational process in what happens in other countries. One recent report from Israel, a nation that stands high on the intellectual scale, describes a quiz given to one hundred Israeli high-school graduates, all over twenty, many of them war veterans. Only thirty-five correctly identified Shakespeare (one said he was a musician); only twenty-two could name five American states;

others listed Canada, Mexico, England, and Russia. *The Last Supper* was identified as a famous quotation, a Chagall picture, a movie, a dessert, and the last meal of condemned men before execution. A dinosaur was identified as a former American President, the incumbent President of Israel, a comet, an American Secretary of State. While the quiz may have been authentic enough, some of the answers cause us to wonder whether the Israeli students could have been exercising their own peculiarly Jewish sense of humor.

From Red China comes a story similar to our own. In a test taken recently by Chinese university graduates employed in scientific and technical jobs, 68 percent failed in mathematics, 70 percent in physics, 76 percent in chemistry. Some of the examinees could not answer a single question in their own specialty, and handed in blank papers. Fortunately for the Chinese ego, it was possible to blame the "Gang of Four" for the debacle. But the people in control were quick to announce a return to the basics that were deemphasized during Mao Tse-tung's Cultural Revolution, when tests and academic requirements for university admission were abolished.

There is a serious side to the problem of education, particularly in its lower reaches, occasioned by the fact that it has finally become common property that Johnny can't read, write, or do simple arithmetic. The blame is spread by the parents on the teachers, by the teachers on home conditions, by social workers on poverty in certain areas, by professors of education on the media, particularly TV, which takes up too much of the children's time. Of course, there is partial justification for all these views. Teachers are far too interested in salary increases, advancement, and union activities; parents are far too permissive; poverty is responsible for unsatisfactory backgrounds; there is far too much TV watching for the children's own good. At the same time, it must also be acknowledged that many of these conditions were in existence in the past. It must also be acknowledged that the older among us tend to overglamorize a past epoch of which we recall the good features and forget the bad.

Frank E. Armbruster, in his book *Our Children's Crippled Future: How American Education Has Failed,* points to the fact that we spend more for education than for national defense: "$75 billion in 1976, more than four times the 1960 figure." Then he goes on to describe how the effectiveness of a school is measured. He gives an account of interviewing the top authority at a top-level conference on the subject, and being told that "you measure performance by how much is spent per capita." To the extent that this system may be in general use, it means that in the mentality of its adepts, just because a good thing may be costly, it follows that a costly thing must be good. But, as they say in the TV ads, "there must be a better way" of determining a school's effectiveness.

The media, which ferret out many things that perhaps should lie undisclosed, often perform a signal service by bringing to light other things that the people really ought to know. Years ago, it was fashionable in educational circles to look with scorn upon the private schools and particularly the parochial schools that flourish in the more poverty-stricken areas of our major cities; this despite the fact that the parochial schools were doing as good a job as the public schools even then, when the public schools were functioning well.

Recently, in a *New York Times* article (October 9, 1977), Edward B. Fiske brought to light the following facts: A comparison of the reading scores from the New York State Education Department with those of eighty parochial schools in the Archdiocese of New York indicates that the latter rank considerably higher. The parochial schools have drawn to themselves large numbers of non-Catholics, of all races and colors, who are interested in getting an education, not in wasting time in a classroom. (Non-Catholics are excused from religious exercises and instruction.) Discipline and respect for authority survive quite well in the parochial schools, and there is a very low incidence of crime. The equipment of the parochial schools is often antiquated, as are the school buildings; but this is more than made up for by the motivation that the teachers succeed in imparting to their charges. Hold your hat for the next item. The average per-pupil cost of elementary parochial schools in the Archdiocese of New York in 1976 was $462; in the public schools it was $2,607. "Moral neutrality," says Eleanor Ford, former superintendent of schools for the Archdiocese, "is the worst thing you can do to a school." So much for the claim that "you measure performance by how much is spent per capita."

Inspired perhaps by the better results achieved in private and sectarian than in public schools, some go so far as to advocate that we abolish the public school system altogether, and replace it with a system of grants and vouchers that will enable parents to enter their children into whatever private school they wish. This is perhaps an extreme view, but a greater liberalization of the voucher system (with proper safeguards, such as making the Regents' exams of New York State mandatory for all schools, private and public) might help the situation.

The charge most frequently heard is aimed at the schools of education, which are said to have turned out far too many Dewey "progressives," who view themselves as agents for political and social change rather than as officers of instruction in factual subjects. This view fails to take into account all the things that have happened and are happening outside the school, not only in the homes and on the streets, but in politics, economics, entertainment, and mores in general.

Perhaps we need a moral rebirth or regeneration that will carry us back to the ideals and methods of the nation's founders, with due allowance made for the changes that have occurred and are occurring. But that is a giant task that must reach into every nook and cranny of society, and will at every step run into the problem of reconciling the freedom of the individual with the needs of society. Are we equal to that task?

Summary

Appearances to the contrary, I have only skimmed the surface of the interaction of the media with a few (by no means all) human activities. The interplay of the old and new media with human greed for money, publicity, or both has been treated only in cross-section style. Far more remains to be said, possibly in another volume, concerning the political rather than the commercial aspects of the situation—the presentation by the media of the language and procedures of the law, the bureaucracy, taxation, party politics, international relations, crime and crime-fighting, finance, labor-capital relations, racial and ethnic problems.

The media, both press and electronic, perform a necessary and useful service—that of providing information and entertainment to those of us who want to be informed and entertained. In performing this service, they are impelled by two primary considerations—sensationalism and the profit motive —which often override everything else. It would be possible to eliminate both by the simple expedient of subjecting the media to totalitarian censorship or full government operation. This would spell the end of liberty and democracy as we know them.

Is there any way of reconciling a system of free enterprise with an improvement in quality? In this connection, it may be of interest to cite the opposing views of three media spokesmen: Fred Silverman, president of ABC Entertainment, joined for the purposes of this discussion by Robert Mandan, creator of the highly controversial TV series "Soap," and Mervin Stone, one of the editors of *U.S. News & World Report*. The first two are representative of the electronic media, the third of the press media.

Speaking to the Hollywood Radio and Television Society, Fred Silverman began by announcing that the primary objective of his station's entertainment programming is to entertain. He criticized the critics who criticize the preferences of one hundred million TV viewers, as indicated by Nielsen ratings for various popular programs ("Laverne and Shirley," "Happy Days," "Charlie's Angels," "Starsky and Hutch," "Baretta" were specifically named). He claimed that ABC was in tune with the contemporary preferences of an overwhelming majority of American TV viewers, reflecting, respecting, and often anticipating those preferences. He went on to scoff at those who accuse that majority of being undiscerning and unsophisticated. "Laverne and Shirley," he continued, according to Nielsen demographics, ranks second nationally in households whose head of the family has had four years of college and earns an income of over $20,000; it ranks first with women aged eighteen to forty-nine, second with men in the same age bracket; it ranks first in households where the head of the family is a professional, owns his own business, or manages a firm. To paraphrase a famous saying, "One hundred million Americans can't be wrong."

Robert Mandan, in an interview with Andee Beck, makes the point that some of his many and vociferous critics may be inspired by the fact that his portrayals of conjugal infidelity strike too close to home for comfort. As for what he calls the "ruckus pressure groups," he accuses them of working a political ploy to gain power over what goes on in TV, and strenuously defends the right of the individual to make his own choices. He scoffs at the idea that TV violence inspires violence in viewers, and cites the case of Lizzie Borden, who carried on her grisly activities at a time when there were no movies, radio or TV, and few newspapers to offer such inspiration. The urge to commit violent acts springs from environmental factors and home conditions, he claims. At any rate, how do we "protect" children and teenagers who today know more about sex than we did at their age? "So what if Rome fell?" he concludes. "The world didn't end. It went on, and it will go on." (True; but it took the better part of a thousand years to stage a comeback.)

Mervin Stone, in an editorial dated November 21, 1977, accuses the networks of searching not for quality but for numbers in the great rating race, giving the public what the public *seems* to want, and outdoing one another in drivel and poor taste. He then goes on to point to the dangers of excessive sex and violence on TV, citing the famous Florida case where a murderer claimed he had been intoxicated by the brutality shown on TV, and to the British BBC's survey indicating that TV is causing an increase in youthful crime. He also deplored the "unrealistic and deceptive force" of TV, citing a case where a psychotic patient hit an employee over the head with a billiard cue and was baffled when the victim did not immediately recover his senses and get up, as happens on TV. The sex shown on the screen, he went on, is too often dismal, selfish, treacherous, animalistic, devoid of tenderness. TV causes many older persons to lead lives of irrational fear of victimization. Congress, he concludes, would take instant notice if a prominent industry pocketed a billion dollars a year in pretax profits while piping sewage into the rivers and lakes. Yet the commercial TV stations pipe their raw "entertainment" garbage into American homes with impunity.

Allowance must be made for the fact that Silverman and Mandan may be consciously or unconsciously inspired by the profit motive in their plea for full freedom of entertainment.

Nielsen ratings of entertainment programs bring commercials to the networks, and commercials are the networks' lifeblood. On the other hand, Stone's weekly magazine boasts in its own TV commercials of having ten million educated, intelligent, mature readers to whom quality appeals. Therefore, a subconscious profit motive cannot be altogether excluded from his presentation, with which most of those select readers will instinctively agree.

An additional point is worth considering, which may supply the key to at least part of the controversy. On the same night, I happened to sit through three programs in their entirety: "Hawaii Five-O" on CBS-TV; "Once upon a Classic: the Legend of Robin Hood" on WNET; and the second episode of "I, Claudius" on the same noncommercial channel.

"Hawaii Five-O" has often been listed as one of the most violent programs on TV, and the charge is to some extent true. Yet on this particular night only one person was killed, and there was no other violence of any kind. "Robin Hood," prepared and announced by the BBC as a "children's program," had at least a dozen killings and other assorted acts of violence. "I, Claudius" had one poisoning, a hint of more to come, and considerable sex (far more of both sex and violence occurred in later episodes, but invariably with the justification that both sex and violence are fully historical, and based on the writings of Suetonius and Tacitus). CBS-TV makes no pretense of being anything but a commercial network, much concerned with ratings and profits. WNET is noncommercial, nonprofit, and highly cultural. But on this occasion (November 18, 1977) it far outstripped CBS in both violence and sex.

This leads me to think that some of the criticism of the commercial networks may be based, first, on their avowed motivation; second, on their defiant attitude; third, on their mode of presentation, as to both style and subject matter. The critics seem disposed to forgive a great deal if the network, first, is nonprofit and unconcerned with ratings; second, offers a generally justified reputation for cultural aims; third, presents programs that might seem objectionable elsewhere, but in graceful, correct style, and with a background of history or tradition. The commercial networks might reply that their style is contemporary and reflects, in large part, present-day mores and history. For the other two points there does not seem to be any suitable disclaimer.

Aside from all this, one might cast some doubts on the validity of the Nielsen ratings, based upon a very limited number of family groups, which, however scientifically selected to represent a cross section of the hundred million viewers, are always the same. One recalls the tremendous gaffe of the *Literary Digest* in connection with the Roosevelt-Landon election campaign of 1936. The magazine, which had always successfully followed the practice of calling up people at random on the phone and asking them which candidate they favored, forgot that in those days, and particularly in the depth of the depression, many members of the lowest-income and unemployed groups had either never had phones or had been forced to give them up. But those phoneless people still went to the polls. Despite the *Digest*'s forecast, Landon got only Maine and Vermont. But today people who are unemployed or on welfare still have phones, so that a more random but wider phone sampling might be more accurate than a Nielsen rating. Also, advertisers might be reminded that TV program watchers are not necessarily buyers of the products mentioned in commercials. While many people fall for the commercials, just as many are uninfluenced or even antagonized (this I know from personal experience).

But even granting full accuracy to Nielsen ratings, all they indicate is a majority preference for certain types of programs. If these are as harmful as claimed by their critics, should this majority preference still be allowed to prevail? There was a time when it was fashionable for a majority of people to smoke.

Then it was conclusively proved that smoking is harmful to the health of the smokers. We did not repeat the mistake of trying to ban smoking by constitutional amendment, as we had tried to ban alcohol. But a relentless campaign of information about the potential harm of smoking began, and continues to this day. Some people gave up smoking; others decreased their tobacco intake; still others refrained from starting the habit. Smoking was banned by laws and regulations from certain places where it had been indiscriminately permitted before, in response to the pleas of nonsmokers who thought they might be affected by other people's smoking.

Without trying to legislate out of existence sex and violence on radio-TV and in the press, is it not legitimate to propagandize the bad effects such programs and publications may have on certain types of minds, and restrict both by appropriate legislation? If viewers who prefer such programs and publications find themselves faced with a shortage of the same, coupled with an improvement in quality and good taste, will they give up their firmly rooted habits of viewing and reading? Will they not rather be impelled to view and read what is widely available? In some totalitarian countries, where both electronic and press media are under control, both politically and from the standpoint of taste, there is little indication of lack of interest in TV, radio, newspapers, books, and magazines.

The legislation, on the federal level because of the interstate nature of the media, would have to be very carefully framed, after full and open discussion, perhaps even be subjected to popular referendum. Most of its aspects would be restrictive rather than prohibitive. Programs featuring excessive sex and violence might be restricted to certain hours and localities, or to specified radio and TV channels, which would be excluded from specially constructed sets designed for the use of children. This might raise the question of constitutionality, on which the Supreme Court should pass promptly and decisively.

The only logical alternative would be to let things follow their present course, and trust to luck, progress, and education to improve quality. This may sound defeatist, but it really isn't. Networks and publishers of newspapers, books, and magazines have already been sufficiently alerted to the groundswell against some of their practices. It is up to them to assume a sense of real responsibility, even at the cost of giving up their senseless race for ratings and inordinate profits. As the British say in their road signs, "You have been warned!"

Peaceful accommodation and compromise, in this as in all things, is preferable to confrontation and a showdown of strength.

One hundred million American viewers may not be wrong, but are there really that many viewers for the programs most objected to? Or that many readers of pornographic materials? Or is there a silent majority that objects to them, but so far has limited itself to peaceful protest?

Index